# Stories of
# ROUND
# TIMBER HAULAGE

Maurice H. Sanders

Cortney Publications, Luton

Published in 1984
by
Cortney Publications,
95-115 Windmill Road, Luton, Beds. LU1 3XS


Reprinted February 1985


ISBN 0 904378 25 X

Cover Illustration by Peter Davies

Inprint of Luton Limited

# Contents

# The Oak

The noisy lorry rattles down the road,
Upon its trailer, as upon a bier,
Lies stretched a mighty Oak, an object drear,
Torn from the hill which nobly it bestrode,
And to the observant eye its beauty showed,
Now, where the waving leaves erstwhile had grown,
A dirty piece of rag tied to its crown,
Flutters a warning of its massive load.

And yet, our sad regrets may be but vain,
With adge and saw the cunning craftsman's art
Reveals to sight the wonderous silver grain
Till now lying hidden in the oaken heart
So loveliness, undying braves all storms,
And is transmuted into other forms.

Ursula G. Wilson

With acknowledgements to 'The Timber Trade Journal' c. 1930.

# The Photographs

The 196 photographs in this book are a major feature. Most of them have never been published, and most of them have been taken by amateur photographers, many of whom were in the "eighty hour week brigade", and had no time to worry about posing refinements. Many come from pre war Kodak Brownie days, delightful snapshots in themselves which when enlarged magnify the defects, leading to many darkroom nightmares!

Three lots were stuck firmly into Family Albums I borrowed complete. A fine Latil shot was jammed in between "Bob and Doll at Clacton", on one side, and "Our Ken's Wedding" the other. One collection had been kept in the cab, stunk to high heaven of diesel, and had to be cleaned up.

Some were rescued from dusty attics where they had been for 40 years or more; several were literally folded in drivers' wallets, and naturally the fold marks are reproduced. Where the reproduction is poor, it is because this may be the *only* copy of any one vehicle. This is not meant as a book of super photographs but rather of illustrations intended to give a better insight into the work and dedication of those wonderful men and women.

Some were understandably reluctant to even loan these treasures, being the only link between their hey-day and the present, when the ravages of time and timber had taken their toll health wise.

I will always remember an old driver now eaten up with arthritis and another grim disease, pointing a trembling finger to a shot of a tough young lad pulling out an inch cable thigh deep in mud and slurry, and saying, as tears ran down his cheeks, "You will never believe that was me".

People ranging from ten years to ninety six have contributed these pictures, hence the great variation.

*IMPORTANT*

Our apologies to those donors, whose snapshot was not used. The choice of picking 196 plus from almost 400 timber scenes was very difficult. I have attempted to cover the timber haulage concept as widely as possible and that has not been easy.

The Author

# Acknowledgements

I wish to acknowledge my thanks and appreciation to the following friends without whose help this book would not have been possible.

To Howard Nunnick who carried his camera all over the north photographing timber operation scenes in the 1960's.

To Jim Macdougall, a 'dyed in the wool' Foden man, who owns a 1946 GHT 6/50 winch tractor and laid his vast knowledge of these timber tractors at my disposal.

To Glen McBirnie whose keen eye for winches of every make, as he travels the country, has kept me informed of them for several years.

To John Murfet for his unique photograph of the Berry road-train.

To Christopher Randall of the Latil Register who has a wealth of information on these vehicles.

To Mr. F. S. Limb of Earls Colne for his insight into the background and set-up of the home timber trade; and for the treasured snapshot of the International tractor that had served so well his old company, T. & A. J. Mann. It was a type of timber tractor I found no trace of anywhere else.

To Chris. Salaman who is not even in timber, yet came up with help in answer to questions which had stumped all the timber men.

To Miss Bette Anderson for contacting old Lumber Jill friends.

To Mr. G. Holbrow of Bradford-on-Avon who, when a timber merchant, used many auto winches including the first V8 engined-Model V and spoke glowingly of this.

To The Rev. C. D. R. Stevens, vicar of Sweffling, who went the second mile seeking local ex-timber men. A picture of a Foden in his Parish Church had taken me there (not that they have canonized this famous Cheshire name). The Church has a magnificent museum containing photographs of the village over the years — seed time, harvest, flood, even timber haulage — it's all there. My thanks are due also to John Powter for reproducing the photographs.

To Cliff Baker, Derek Lugo, George Chandler, Sam Newson and Jack Gospel who all helped so much with photographs and vehicle history.

To Mr. Esmond Harris director of the Royal Forestry Society for access to the exceptional library at Tring and for all his friendly guidance.

To Mr. W. J. Wilson who sent Forestry Commission photographs and named so many other people who have helped.

To Mr. Peter Scott and Mr. G. R. Dodd of T. H. White Ltd of Frome for access to the Auto-Mower Archives.

To my old friend George Reynolds and his Merry Men for personal Auto-Mower background.

To Mrs. L. Perridge who cut out and passed on the poem, 'The Oak'.

To Dorothy Tuffnell who tended and nurtured the idea of this book whenever it seemed to wilt.

To Ron Ward for all his gifted photographic work, particularly in reproducing dog-eared snapshots that had been folded in drivers' wallets for years.

To my good friend Ben Hinton who ferried treasured photographs hundreds of miles, carried out interviews and did so much behind the scenes.

To Peter Davies for his excellent Cover Illustration, which is based on a photograph loaned by Peter Berry of Saxmundham.

To Norman Gurney of Cortney Publications who backed the book all the others threw out, and Stanley Carter of Luton whose editing did much to improve its literary standard.

To all those who participated in loaning photographs and giving unstintingly of their time.

––––––––––––––

A story is told of an old gardener who won first prize with selected fruit at a local show. Eyebrows were raised when he gave a list of names to substitute his own on the award card, Unashamedly he explained, "None of these fruits are mine. I only gathered and brought them for people who just never seemed to get round to showing them for themselves". So it is that none of these fruits are mine for, like the gardener of old, they are from folk who never got round to showing them off themselves.

––––––––––––––

# Glossary

ANCHORS — A large spade or sprag mounted on the rear (generally) of a tractor to hold the machine whilst roping.

ARTIC — Articulated.

C HOOK — A hardened hook shaped like the letter C used extensively until the advent of the hydraulic loader for quick fastening of a winch rope to a chain or sling.

CLEATS or SPUDS — Various metal bars that are fixed to drive wheels for extra traction in wet conditions.

CUBE — A cubic foot of round timber assessed by the use of the HOPPUS ready reckoner measure used by timber men for over one hundred years. Approximately 25 cubic feet of green hardwood weigh about a ton.

DOUBLE HEADING — The practise of two outfits running together and at the foot of a steep hill one tractor unhitching its trailer and leaving it, then it would hook onto the other loaded unit for extra pull up the hill. After which both units would return to the other load and bring that up likewise.

DRUG — Another name for pole waggon or timber carriage.

GRADIENT GLOW — The 'red hot' effect a steep hill had on some exhaust manifolds, and on brake drums descending same; most obvious at night!

KETTLE WEDGE — Name given to a wood chip axed out by fallers setting up a tree. (Ideal for firewood).

LODGER — The act of one tree falling into another when felling, in a big tree often dangerous to move. Frequently nicknamed 'a widow maker'.

QUAD — Light ex-army Gun-tractor,

SKIDS & 3 LEGS — Skids — wooden (preferably ash) support ramps used previously for loading; 3 legs or Shear legs previously used mostly in Wales and the North.

SNATCH BLOCK — Pulley for increasing pull.

SHEFFIELD BLIGHT — Description given to severely lopped tree. (Steel butchery).

TIDY STICK — Big tree.

THROWERS — West Country name for fallers.

TUSHING or SNIGGING — Term for extracting or pulling out trees to point of loading.

TWITCH — GIRTING IRON — WRISTER — WITTERING STICK — Local names given to a load binder that tensions loading chains in transit.

ZIG-ZAGGING — A somewhat dangerous, but at one time an accepted practice of climbing a steep hill, when overloaded, by crossing over from one side of the road to the other.

# Introduction

The author was employed as a round timber haulier from demobilization in 1946 and into the fifties. His thirty years in timber have proved every aspect is hard and tough, even down to trying to produce a book about it. For the most part, meeting people for this publication has been fascinating, a pleasure, and sometimes even a humbling honour. The saddest part was learning of the high number of accidents that abound among men and women in timber. The looking up of old friends and places and recording conversations was done over a period of four years. I am most indebted for the time and immense help given to me by the participants.

Moving trees is a most dangerous calling. Many a man has paid dearly for a wrong decision of his own or his mates. In the woods, one was required to select, extract and load by means of skids or three legs: an acquired skill prior to jibs spoiling us. A big tree that was loaded wrongly could smash and write off a pole trailer in a moment. As trees differ in their nature, so do the problems of felling. For instance, you may have a lodger or tushing out may be fraught with stumps and obstacles. On the road, the outfit which might have been around forty-feet long unloaded could have at times another twenty or more feet added to that. Immediately, a number of hazards, unknown to other drivers, became apparent, from mud on the road, shop blinds inches over the kerbside, to traffic bollards waiting to catch one's red, ragged tree-tails, on a journey that could be as long as three to three hundred miles. In fairness, the police themselves often appeared uncertain of the law concerning log carting, generally giving us the benefit of the doubt. We all grumbled about getting soaked to the skin and frosts that made the chains stick to the fingers, yet once timber got in the blood, few would pursue a different living.

To speed the supply of wood during the Second World War, the Ministry of Supply, Home Timber Production Dept., made well over 500 vehicles available to the trade on a lease basis. I am told that Registration letters — HAE, HHT, HHU, HHW, HHY and JAE were among those used. The makes included Unipower, Foden, ERF, Albion, Bedford, Ford, Austin, International, and FWD. Eventually, some vehicles were offered for purchase to the leaseholders. Others found their way to the North German Timber Control (B.A.O.R.)

In the 1940-1960s, pole trailers were as common as skip-trucks today. It was possible to stand at the top of a sprawling hill on Salisbury Plain and at a given time see eight or nine sets of tackle wending their big, long loads easterly under such names as T. T. Boughton, F. Honour, Judd, Charlton, Sadd, Chalk, Fensom, and others. A whole chorus of notes rose from the full-throated sounds of Gardner 5 and 6's, AEC's and Leyland engines running high as they took yet another incline in low or super-low gear.

As an old character, nicknamed 'Hoppy Gates', once said to a policeman, when a chain had broken, causing a tree to half fall off in the busy High Street of a market town, "Yes, officer, I can understand the lady having to jump for her life. Very wise of her. I've always said you never know what a tree is going to do".

*This was Timber Hauling*

# Steaming from Exeter to Sweffling

In 1921, at the age of nineteen, Alec. K. Cooper was driving a Burrell Steam Tractor belonging to his father's threshing business in Sweffling, Suffolk. Young Alec was engaged in pulling out felled timber at nearby Peashall. He remembers how they only felled in winter and that trees lay in the sawmill yard drying in a five year rotation. As he developed timber hauling on his own, he recalls vividly going down to Claridges of Exeter to purchase and drive home a Foden Steam Tractor, covering around a hundred miles a day and sleeping at times in the coal bunker. In 1933, he bought his first Latil, a KTL Model with a canvas top, the first of many Latils to come to Sweffling.

A natural progression was to Unipowers after Latils, by which time several sets of tackle regularly worked in the whole of East Anglia and the Home Counties. Caterpillar D6s and D7s were used for extractions on the big jobs. Two or three of these did valiant service clearing up in 1953 after the East Coast Flood disaster.

Alec. K. Cooper's trickiest job was not in timber at all, but on the occasion when a giant cylinder was to be installed in a local malting establishment and it was found that there was no room to off-load it from a low loader on site. Much planning went into making up front and rear dollies from timber carriage turntables. Thus, with a Latil in front and a Unipower pushing they made their way through the narrow street right into the required position, with the Latil being able to turn out from its tight corner by a matter of inches, thanks to four-wheel steering.

Much of Cooper's success was due to the good workshop back-up where, at times, they rebuilt tractors for other companies. In 1968, the business was sold, consisting finally of updated vehicles including Douglas and Matadors all fitted with Unipower winches.

Alec Cooper went to the Gold Coast of Africa where he had exported Caterpillar Tractors and Matadors. Here he saw them at work pulling huge trees out of the bush up to a road a mile away. He had second thoughts about his plan to set up timber hauling out there when, at times, he saw some twenty natives loading trees by pulling on a rope instead of using the traditional winches.

Today, Alec Cooper relives his days in timber haulage. He is actively engaged now in pig farming, claiming, even at eighty, that this occupation has less blood, sweat and tears than log carting. Doubtless, the dire situation of the present pig industry would alter his thoughts. Surely, timber haulage was never bedevilled with such problems. 'Cooper Happy Family' proclaims the chalked sign on the photograph of the living-van, (taken at kettle-wedge time), embodying a feeling that lives on with the ex-Suffolk timber men I met, even after sixteen years.

1

*The Foden Mr. Cooper drove home from Exeter*

*Moving ashphalt plant with a Police escort*

*The Latil Lads*

*Alec Cooper's trickiest job*

*Cooper's happy family*

*Driver's mate Derek Lugo in Woburn Park*

*Bill Newson in action*

*A mishap on the A12*

*Cliff Baker with the last Unipower*

4

*A.K. Cooper with a friend!*

Courtesy of Sweffling Church Museum

5

# Fred Stannard

A. K. Cooper of Sweffling advertised for a crawler driver and Fred Stannard went after the job. He couldn't drive a crawler; in fact, in all honesty, he'd not even seen one. However, he was offered tuition and a fortnight's trial. "That was at the time of the Chamberlain crisis", said Fred, "and I stayed with Mr. Cooper until he retired in 1968. He never did say if the trial was favourable."

"I lived at Spexhall then, fifteen miles away, that meant a thirty mile a day push-bike ride, save when I was away on a job. It was war-time then and grub was short, so we used to snare a rabbit or two and later I bought a four-ten shot gun. Before I got a proper living van, I had lodging money, but saved it by living in a little bivouac tent". Fred produced a picture of sheeting hung over a frame on a little trailer used for towing the crawler's forty-gallon diesel drum around. "I lived in there six months", Fred boasted. "I remember once we were on some earl's estate when he came round at supper time. The aroma from the black pot on the fire caused the earl to bend forward to observe the potatoes and carrots bubbling below and sniffing he remarked, 'My word your folk look after you well'. It didn't occur to him that it was his people looking after Fred, who could recommend the earl's kitchen-garden most highly. One evening Fred's mate, Tom, was almost ready with the rabbit stew, giving it the final stir, when Fred required him urgently with the crawler. A little lad who was looking on offered to take on the stirring. On his return, Tom loaded Fred's plate with lashings of veg, gravy and meaty rabbit leg. He then commenced to fish in the pot for his own portion of bunny. His look of anticipation turned to despair as he saw the lad disappearing hurriedly. 'Blast that boy he's eaten my rabbit's leg', he exploded. He did carry on.

"When we had to move sites, Jackson's, the land draining people, often did it with their old Albion, a high old lorry with almost bare chassis. It was all right if there was a bank to load from, which was seldom, but a bit risky otherwise. No matter how we blocked the back up, it would move just as you reached the point of balance when loading the old Fowler I was driving then. This would rear up the old Albion in the air and keep her thus until she went down with a hell of a bang as I tracked on. She was a good old lorry. Not many would stand that as often as she did. The Albion had no coupling so we used to chain the diesel trailer on to the back. One day, after loading, I went on ahead to the next job on the old motor bike I'd got then and waited for ages. In the end, I tracked back to find that when the old Albion was going up an embankment, the trailer had become unchained and charged to the foot of the incline tipping over as it came to rest. There was the diesel, my old tent, plates, kettles, saucepans and tin mugs scattered everywhere. We found all our stuff, bar the frying pan, and to this day we don't know where that went."

"Then came the living vans which would often accommodate five or six, counting the fallers, sleeping on bags of clean straw. When we came home on Saturday mornings for the weekend, I've sat the six of us on the back of the tractor in the pouring rain, perhaps all the way from Leicester. One night we were coming home from Ipswich along the A12. I was sitting in the box on the back of a Latil and I called to the driver, old Bill Newson, saying, 'We've got no rear light and someone nearly hit us'. 'All right', said Bill. He just let the winch-brake off a notch so that the anchors touched the road occasionally as the old tractor rocked along. Every few moments

6

that put up a shower of sparks that lit up the Latil like a damn great firework. It got us home safely even if it did ground his anchor points a bit. Pity you never knew Bill Newson. He was a master man with a Latil. You will know that to drive a Latil, you should be an all-in wrestler. You will remember how they first pull one way, then the other as you drive along. Well, I was just outside Framlingham once when the one I was driving stopped doing that. The fact is that it stopped steering altogether. The drop-arm had dropped off. I went in the ditch, the steering wheel spokes all broke, and I was still holding the wheel as it went down on the floor. That knocked off three of the four wheels and wrecked it."

Next Fred had a petrol-engined Unipower, the fastest tractor in the yard. He said, "I could go up to Stevenage with a load, return, and put another load on in a day — she could go it." One special job Fred had was to move some seventy-two feet of imported Douglas Fir for a special job in Bury St. Edmunds, with only two inches clearance at one point of the journey.

Fred was once sent to a quarry with a Matador to pull out a Motor Grader. That was eight o'clock one morning. On seeing nothing in the water, he queried if he had the right location. The driver assured him he was right as he pointed to something black just above the water. "That's the top of the cab", he explained. "Well then," said Fred, "that's going to take two if not three Matadors to get that out." In the end it took four, all with snatch-blocks in bottom gear working in unison and it was just eight o'clock that night when the Grader finally surfaced.

Few crawler drivers make the front page of the National Newspapers, but Fred did. Back in January 1960, a large Coaster ran aground at Bawdsey, Suffolk in a snowstorm. Fred was sent with a D6, working for three days against the tides bulldozing tons of shingle to facilitate refloating the vessel before storms broke her up. He is proud of that cutting.

Fred and his mate took a very awkward load of mixed timber into a yard one day, when to make matters worse and treble the unloading time, the owner said, "I want all the long ones unloading here and all the short ones over there". Fred's mate's patience ran out and he said rather loudly, "I'll tell you where he wants this load". On hearing this, the timber merchant turned and said, "Oh, where do I want this load?" to which came the hurried reply, "The long ones here and the short ones over there."

While we laugh with Fred Stannard, as this droll son of Suffolk relives those grim war times, it is worth remembering that he and his like battled, not only against the elements of weather and stubborn trees, but also against serious shortages of fuel and food. During the war when both were rationed, it took many signatures on a form to get a manual worker a mite extra cheese, to say nothing of a drop more petrol or diesel. Yet these vast East Anglian airfields were being cleared ready for the USA Air Force almost around the clock and all timber was at a premium and on licence. It was said that something like nineteen thousand men alone were involved in building the famous much-wooded construction Mulberry Harbour for the second front and the timber was kept available at all times. This is just one example of the role of wood during the war and many people felt that the timber-man was on a par with the munition-worker in the importance of his contribution to the war effort. In any story of tree work, Fred Stannard and his sort must surely have a place.

*A tense moment for Fred Stannard*

*Fred with the Fowler*

*This must be the first camping trailer*

*Great Glemham — a winter scene*

8

# From Poplars to pop groups

When the writer called on Jim Berry, buyer of standing timber and haulier of Framlingham, Suffolk, back in April, 1983, he was inspecting the latest acquisition to his fleet delivered that day, Reg. No. FVG 488Y, a Volvo rigid 8 wheeler, self loader, a wonderful vehicle. A Leyland Marathon 8 wheeler, a Leyland Road Train and a Scania Tractor Unit with ballast box ran with two independent 6 wheel pole trailers alternatively at one time. If in this day of the artic. you think this was a retrograde step, remember Jim ran these as a shuttle and found the idea profitable. These and other vehicles are driven by three of Jim's sons, George, Peter and Paul, who deliver the timber that Jim buys, possibly loaded by either the first Volvo BM Hydraulic Loader in East Anglia, which Jim pioneered, or by the latest centrally articulated Volvo loader.

In a time when the home timber trade is contracting, the "Berry Story" is encouraging. When fourteen and a half years old, Jim and his brother Peter lost their father who was killed in the pursuance of his job, timber hauling. This grim start to life did nothing to deter either of the boys who sought a living with trees. Now it is to Peter, in business on his own account as a faller and specialist in dangerous tree work, that we are indebted for so many photographs from his collection. He brought along some two hundred. Peter Berry would no more think of going to work without his camera than without his sandwich box and no more expect to run out of film than out of chain-saw oil. He must be Kodak's favourite man in Suffolk.

When he was about fifteen years old, Jim started work with none other than A. K. Cooper, whose own story is featured elsewhere in this book. Jim got a good grounding in pulling out, loading, and hauling. Would that there were room to retell the fund of stories Jim recalls. He spent a good deal of time in a living-van on distant jobs and was frequently the junior lad to one of the older caterpillar drivers, Fred Stannard — one of the old brigade. He recalled how when Fred's D6 was in the yard for repair, as he was some way from his home, Fred continued to live in the van and used the occasion not only to stock up well with coal for the van's stove, but to hoard and stow such amounts in various concealed places that the weight of the van was greatly increased. On the first day out, Fred was towing the van with the D6 up a slippery slope when the spinning tracks jerked the van drawbar off the C hook, whereupon the van, heavily laden with coal, ran backwards, overturned and deposited its contents everywhere. It looked like a coalyard when Jim arrived with a Latil for the recovery operations. Unperturbed, Fred had made a fire while he waited and greeted him with, "How do you like your sausages, Jim?" It was quite legal to tow a van from the pole of a timber drug providing two men were in attendance with the driver and Jim recalls the odd sensation of riding at the rear some fifty feet from the Latil, especially at times of cornering. One very hot summer, before the days of foot-deodorant, Jim recollected how Fred had sniffed and ordered him in his broad Suffolk dialect, "Do you take out your socks and hang them underneath on the axle, I'm not having them in here". Once, in London, Jim was with a Latil and unloaded drug when they entered a police speed trap. On being waved down, it took them some sixty yards or so to pull up. The police, thinking they were not stopping, gave chase with a car. It seems they had recorded a speed of 27 mph (seven over the limit). The police put the long stopping distance down to the driver's interest in the safety of other road users and not to his inability to stop. They were let off with a caution.

It takes two to use a crosscut: or does it? Jim got married when he was twenty and had the urge to branch out on his own. Only the lack of money stood in his way, but not for long. Armed with only a pushbike, a crosscut saw, and a piece of catapult elastic, Jim set out from farm to farm. Each time he used the same approach, "I have no money to buy your tree outright, but if you will trust me I will fell it, get it hauled to the sawmill, and pay you an agreed price when they pay me". Now in all the time Jim did this, not once did he fail to pay the farmer, not once did a farmer refuse to trust him. If knowing farmers raises any doubt in your mind, knowing Jim Berry would quell it, for as well as his bike, saw and elastic, he had one other far greater asset, integrity, and it was going to be his greatest aid in future business. "But where does the elastic come in?" you ask. Jim remembers once, as a boy, seeing an old man crosscutting on his own and got the idea of using elastic as a second person in the felling operation. Having chopped the fall in a tree, he would remove a handle from his six-foot Diston saw and with a skewer fix his length of catapult-elastic, choosing a place just forward of the cut and, giving the tension, he anchored the other end to an iron stake driven in the ground. Moving the stake as he proceeded to cut, Jim discovered he could fell a tree single-handed, even up to forty-five quarter girth on occasions. When funds permitted, Jim bought an old Morris car in order to go further afield. In fact, in 1952 he went down to Barnstaple in Devon felling for Pye's of Elmswell.

He often worked with Peter, who in later years was also with A. K. Cooper, who often loaned him a tractor for pulling their trees. Jim's first tractor, No. 186LBJ, was one of the ten shortened Matadors that AKC had fitted with Unipower winches. It stands today on the button beside Jim's house for emergency pulling. A second Matador and two six-wheeled drugs were purchased by Jim when Mr. Cooper retired in 1968.

Jim told me of the fury of railway officials who, when trees were being unloaded in a goods yard, caught redhanded a driver who first snatch-blocked on to the rails and afterwards attempted to realign the bent track with his anchors.

In the grim winter of 1963, Jim finally bought a black Italian Poplar that stood on an island in a river whose waters must have swelled the great tree. It had been offered for sale long before that year, but no summer had ever dried out the marshy ground enough or winter ever frozen it enough to enable it to be felled and hauled out. That was not until 1963. These photographs show Jim and Peter with a Douglas getting it out. They had walked across the ice, the thickness of which was great enough to bear the giant tree's weight. At one stage, one Matador virtually held the other one down whilst roping. The tree had 735 cubic feet in the first length and the loaded drug stood on a lay-by for two weeks before the roads could be travelled. No wonder all the family turned out to see it.

From poplars to pop groups — One of Peter's photographs featured a Bedford Dormobile, which while carrying a pop group was badly impaled on the pole of a timber drug. While Jim and Peter were doing a roadside felling job, the drug was parked awaiting the tree. It seeems that as the group driver approached, he was looking up in the tree at the lopping operation, when the group was rudely joined in the cab by the last three feet of the drug's pole. The impact caused the rear door to fly

10

open and out blew a large fur coat, which was taken by a gust of wind across the road. For one awful moment, Jim, who saw the incident, thought the coat was occupied. Happily it was not.

Today, Jim still occupies half of the old A. K. Cooper yard at Sweffling, where I paused for a few moments recollecting how it had been built around such great names as Burrell, Foden, Fowler, Caterpillar, Latil, Unipower and AEC, names of a great past giving way now to Leyland and Volvo. At that moment, Jim's other brother, George, turned into the yard with the giant articulated Volvo loader. Progress indeed, showing that they are making sure the logs will keep rolling in and out of Sweffling.

*The Leyland road train*

*A Matador held the Douglas down as she roped out this tree*

*The twins top a load*

*Jim's one man cross cut saw*

*Peter Berry captures a good load*

*The 750 cube poplar (1963)*

*Human counter weight*

12

# Boy with a Brownie

Someone gave young Peter Chilvers a Kodak Brownie Box Camera for his birthday. Keen to try it out, he looked round his village in Rendham, Suffolk for the makings of a good picture.

They were loading timber up in the marshes, an all too common scene, but, to Peter's surprise, they were doing it without the usual horse team or steam engine. Instead, they had a small but powerful motor tractor with its own winch. It was a French machine called a Latil, one of the first in those parts, the men with it told the lad. Peter took a few very good shots and even noted down the men's names, Bill Newson and Wesley Neale. There's youthful enthusiasm for you.

Peter was thrilled with his efforts and when shortly after that a new farming paper to be called the "Farmer's Weekly" appeared and as an opening interest feature ran a farm photographic contest, he entered a Latil snapshot. This won him five shillings and fame in the new magazine, which published the photograph and headed it, "Timber Hauling the Modern Way". He didn't dream that fifty years on someone would cross half of England to bring you these excellent close-up shots of a Latil in a book.

Mr. Peter Chilvers is a retired farmer now living in Badingham. He also has a most fascinating collection of rural photography that is a joy to behold. What a good job someone gave young Peter that camera and that we can all enjoy his efforts long after the Latil, Bill and Wesley are gone!

*The first Latil to come to Sweffling*

*Bill Newson and Wesley Neale*

13

*Tushing out*

*Winching in*

# Star for a day

I found Sam Newson in The Ivy House at Stradbroke in Suffolk. He had not come to the inn for a drink, but is the publican there. The Rev. C. D. Stevens of Sweffling's appeal for timber-men's memories had caught his eye. Sam had more A. K. Cooper photographs and a unique one featuring the old chain-drive TG5 Foden owned by Wheeler's of Sudbury. Sam often hauled into their yard and knew well both the Foden and driver.

At one time, Sam was on a petrol-engined Unipower. This tractor should have been called 'The Sweffling Flyer' since it would reach 55 miles per hour with ease. If you don't think that is fast, remember that the Gardner-engined versions cut out at around twenty-five (unless doctored) and anyway at that time a good many cars did not do much more than that. Much of Sam's time was spent hauling from Northamptonshire and the East Midlands, chiefly on large estates.

He did not plan to be a film star, but he became one if only for a day. When they were hauling from Assington near Sudbury, he and his mate often mused over a huge Cedar of Lebanon growing there. They even discussed how they would go about loading such a tree, little knowing that years later this giant tree would be felled and prior to sawmilling would be used for exhibition purposes at the Royal Show in Blackpool. A film unit was commissioned whose job it was to cover the felling and then the loading of this tree. It was not the biggest tree ever to be loaded, but certainly it was one of the trickiest. The strict orders to both drivers and mates of the Unipower and Douglas were that during the loading operation no bark was to be knocked off the trunk for appearance's sake. Therefore Bailey Bridge sections were used in lieu of skids and thickly covered with straw, as were the bolsters. Enlightened readers will know the responsibility that lay with the two loaders. This tidy stick had to go up right first time and no amount of slewing or uneven turning on a block would do. It would appear she loaded well or else some time was spent nailing the bark back on the tree. It has been known.

Sam Newson pulls pints now. Old timber men, who want a yarn and the chance of a bit of "over the bar" timber haulage, should call at this Stradbroke public house. Verbal tree work is a lot less exhausting and nowhere near as dangerous as the real thing. Ask Sam, he can tell you.

*All set for the Royal Show at Blackpool*

*Wheeler's of Sudbury TG5 Foden*

*A tidy stick!*

*Loading the big cedar*

*One of the many Cooper Unipowers*

*Chopping off a spur*

16

# Oscar and the Tulip Tree

Oscar Kettle is smiling, and so should the owner of this rare Tulip tree be. Tulip trees are noted for their beautiful grain. "Where my caravan has rested, went the old song. There is an ex A. K. Cooper living-van in Oscar's garden, less its wheels and which is covered with foliage now. During its travels it slept six at a time and it still has the original stove and sink.

Timber is in his wife's blood, too. The marvellous horse scene was taken at Watton, Norfolk. Her grandfather, John Smith, the one with the beard, was in charge of the operation and was well known in his day, the early 1900s.

*Oscar and the Tulip Tree*

*Watton Norfolk*

# Maggie and Shula

Leslie Tite of Long Sutton, near Basingstoke, bought a double-decker bus to expand the growing timber business that he had started. A double-decker bus seems a strange choice, but it proved to be the right one, with dual duties, both as a low loader to transport the ex-WD Quad and all the bulky charcoal-burning kilns around the woods of Surrey, Sussex and Hampshire, as well as delivering the large bags of charcoal stacked up seven-ton loads at a time. The main customer was ICI who used the charcoal for making cyanide, gun powder and many medical requisites. That old 1939 Leyland must have felt the contrast of her new role to her working life in Birmingham. Leslie first cut away all the body, less the cab. The chassis end dipped a little to form a natural beaver tail, but never worsened after that. A Chev. and Canadian Ford V8 were used to cart out the cordwood and, like the bus, worked for years and years.

Leslie's first round timber haulage vehicle was a six-wheeled Matador, a bolster wagon carrying about 400 cubic feet, loaded with his home-made crane-cum-logging arch. Bigger, longer loads were the order of the day. Leslie's adaptive initiative got to work again, buying and shortening one of the many ex-RN six-wheeled Fodens and making up his own articulated pole trailer from a giant ex-USA Shula tank transporter, a 50 ton unit whose eight $14 \times 20$ wheels were over the legal width until they were reorganised.

A Scammel compressor on the Fodens 6 LW supplied the air for the trailer, thus making a super outfit that would carry 600 to 800 cubic feet with tree lengths up to eighty feet at times, on long hauls to Leeds, Plymouth and Norfolk, for example. The unit worked well and the Foden brought nothing but praise, so in due course Leslie ordered a brand new six-wheeled Foden with a Cummins 220 and waited, but each time the delivery date came round, Foden's put it back and back. Now it so happened that a friend, who was a Magirus Deutz dealer, came along with a six-wheeled demonstrator, the first of its kind, 235 hp V10 air-cooled with splitter box. The 'Maggie' and the Shula took to each other from the word go, loaded or light, far or near, they halved the running time and 'Maggie' became a hit. Several FWD's served, one equipped with a twenty-two feet extending jib under which one could turn a fair tree. This machine could be made extra stable by the fitting of twin $14 \times 20$ wheels at the back making it eleven feet wide, but water-logged ground held no fears for this lady.

The next challenge came when Leslie was asked to remove hundreds of London's dying elms, not only the easy ones in the parks, but those in the shopping precincts between flats, in hospital grounds and in cul-de-sacs. In fact, from places that were the very essence of inaccessibility. How would you tackle this task? Here is Leslie Tite's recipe. First take an ex WD AEC Militant $6 \times 6$ and shorten it by cutting off the rear axle. Next, fit a 760 Mandator engine, gear box and rear axle, next, a Garwood winch and anchor, mount a five ton Hiab and Lister power pack, build a platform area on which to lower the cut tree lengths, and hitch the tractor to a made-up, short, heavy-duty drawbar-trailer which can be either loaded direct or by travelling out from tight spots with a loaded platform. Do that and you have a machine that did its original job perfectly as it does today when required.

With the advent of the 'wood-burning' stove, Leslie has renewed his interest in bulk cordwood for logs. Looking at the bewildering choice of log splitters on the market left him cold when he wanted a good one. His requirements were a splitter that would penetrate the toughest knot-ridden grain yet be completely mobile. So what did he do? You've guessed it. He made one. He bought a Dennis refuse-collector that crunched up the rubbish and rechanneled the machine's powerful hydraulics to split the biggest logs. First, the Dennis underwent the now famous Tite wheelbase-shortening process. What other machine can travel at 40 mph on the road and offer such splitting muscle? Few, I would imagine.

The shortage of equipment and money in the 1950's bred many ingenious adapters and converters in the timber trade. They were resourceful men of great ingenuity and Leslie Tite is one of these.

*The cut down double decker low loader*

*The ex R.N. Foden and Shula tank transporter bogie*

*Maggie and Shula*

19

*Front View*                    *The converted AEC Militant*                    *Rear View*

*The Foden two stroke eight Legger*

*The Dennis (ex dustcart) Log Splitter. Note the twin 14 × 20's on the Bray — ex FWD*

# Joe and Douglas

Joe Meekin's father could put a tidy load on a timber wagon. He is seen here in two photographs with Burrell Steam Tractors when he worked for Pye's of Elmswell in Suffolk, established over a hundred years ago. It is not surprising that Joe went with dad at fourteen and learned his hauling craft starting with a Foden D Type Steam Tractor and giving thirty-eight years service to the firm and later to R. & R. S. Pye, the brother and sister who succeeded their father in the business. Robert Pye had retired, but at seventy-eight was tragically killed in a road accident at about the time I was researching the Suffolk timber story. His widow, Mrs. Pye, produced the photographs and Joe Meekins gave the commentary. Joe told me that Robert and his sister, Ruby, had run a thriving sawmill at Elmswell. Timber came in from all over the country including Wales.

After a variety of steamers, Joe drove a unique vehicle, a first World War Latil, imported from France. It drove on four large cast iron wheels with differential locks and a six-cylinder French engine. Its anchor was mounted midships, ratchet operated. It had a capstan winch which Pye's replaced with a normal drum winch and they fitted a jib. Joe recalled with relish how versatile the machine was for its day. Next came the standard Latils as we knew them. He remembers the front counterweight bolts breaking, allowing the weights to fall and pitch under the axle, sending him into the ditch. However, he must have landed smoothly since an eight-wheeler retrieved him with a chain without damage. Bob Pye had two Unipowers. One he fitted with a Perkins P6, which made it almost fly they say. However, he was constantly seeking larger tackle and with the advent of ex-army sales after the war became one of the first to try AEC Matadors as timber winch tractors. At this time, Mr. F. L. Douglas of Cheltenham was starting a business of shortening Matadors and building jibs and anchors. He and Bob Pye met and became firm friends. Bob and Joe frequently visited Cheltenham to give development advice and carried out much field-testing for all Douglas equipment, so it is not surprising that the first official Douglas tractor went to Pye's of Elmswell, as did many others when the larger 9.6 engine became available. In their heyday there were five units equipped with five Douglas drugs.

One Pye speciality was bark peeling for tanning. During only six weeks of the year can oak be peeled. Joe frequently took a Douglas, with a special flat-bed body fitted on the bolsters of his drug, up to the tanneries in Northallerton, Yorkshire. Another special contract was moving large fuel tanks from USA air bases. They measured thirty feet long by nine feet wide and they moved over six hundred of these right across the country. It was Pye's success in moving these tanks so safely that led to their getting the contract to winch out of the ground much larger tanks sixty feet long and twelve feet wide. This was a highly skilled job that Joe was in charge of. He often had to use three tractors on one tank. One other vehicle Joe held in high esteem was a USA Ward La France with front and rear mounted winches. He said the vehicle would pull amazing weights just on its brakes alone.

When Bob Pye retired, Joe stayed with the new boss, who is now hauling timber the 1983 way. Joe's current vehicle is almost an updated Douglas since it is an AEC Mandator fitted with Matador running gear and a Gardner 150 engine. On Joe's living room wall hangs a Queen's Award for long service as a part-time fireman, but that's another story. One thing is for sure, if the Queen ever gave an award for "hours at the wheel of a Douglas Timber Tractor", Joe Meekins of Elmswell would be the first to qualify.

*An early load into Pye of Elmswell*

*Joe's father with a Burrell*

*Joe with the Ward La France*

22

*Joe and his mate poise for the camera*

*One of Pye's five Douglas Loggers*

*Joe winches out one of the U.S.A. fuel tanks, size 30′ × 9′*

# All from a box of coins

In 1916, Eric Whatton of Hartwell, Northants, was only twelve and a half years old. Times were hard and his father made him a business proposition, not in so many words, perhaps, but, with an eye on the golden syrup tin Eric kept his money in. He said, "Lend me your savings to put with mine to buy a horse and I'll get a permit for you to leave school at once. We'll go up to Gayhurst Woods. I'll cut faggots and you can take them round the villages to sell". Now Eric loved horses and one was duly bought from nearby Piddington. The receipt hangs in Eric's office today. From this point, the Whattons were in business. Soon they were cutting wood for cotton bobbins and numerous small articles, all sawn by hand. Eric has often demonstrated pit-sawing, although this was used before his time, and he recalls how the sawyer would stretch a line the length of a tree, rub it with chalk, twang it, then follow the mark with a perfect cut, all for a few pence a day.

An old rackbench now adorned their little yard. Other horses followed and a passing memory of horse-haulage is a recollection of four horses pulling with all their strength to load a big elm when a knot fouled the skid. One horse lost its grip and the tree rolled back pulling the four horses into a floundering heap on the ground, like a beaten tug of war team.

Their first motor vehicle was a Model T Ford lorry, an innovation they thought the world of as Lizzie brought home the round butts and took out the sawn timber. One day, when the load was a little on the long side, Eric went to crank up the handle and the whole vehicle reared up several feet into the air. Did they unload? Not a bit of it, but just sawed off lengths from the tail until, with the balance restored, down she came and off they drove. The Ford was followed by a new Bean lorry, a make for which Eric had the highest regard. In 1935, GL3047, the first new Latil, was purchased. Eric drove it home from the Albert Embankment getting used to the vehicles odd crab-like, four-wheel steering in the thickest of London's traffic.

By now, Eric's brothers, Archie and Bob, and later, his own son, had all joined the company. Soon the Whattons knew that they really needed an articulated unit for haulage and they soon got busy designing their own. A blacksmith built a turntable and bolsters on a secondhand Bedford chassis, all complete with an independent brake. Their first artic. was on the road and gave miles of valiant service. All this time, the mill was growing, but the many additional saws at different stages were not really economical and it was Eric's son who pioneered the idea of a completely new mill. Eventually, they favoured a Belgium make which at the time offered more than its rivals. A deal was struck, the old mill stripped out and the revolutionary new mill with thirty motors and many conveyors, all operated from one console, began to work, and was looked upon with envy by many fellow mill-owners.

The hunger for timber was now being met by two purpose-built Maudslay pole wagons plus two other Latils that had come on the scene. On the larger jobs, Caterpillar tractors D6 and D7 pulled out the timber coupled to another Whatton first, a USA imported caterpillar logging arch. Many an estate owner enthused over the reduced ground-damage and the saw-doctor rejoiced to see the cleaner butts.

Brother Archie took over the first Latil and drove her most of her working life, hauling from all over Bucks and Northants. He frequently took her to the London Docks with loads.

The first vehicle in the big time was ERF No. CRV581, a six-wheeled pole unit pictured here with Mr. Whatton, Snr. and a rare olive ash. Later, two new Fodens came along. Here we see a very large butt coming out of Althorp Park. This fine AEC outfit had a trailer made up to Eric Whatton's specifications. AEC supplied the twin rear-wheels and axles, of dumper origin, the trailer was plated and its name plate bore the Whatton name and the wording No. 1. This original plate now adorns Eric's fireside, as does a Latil radiator badge.

Probably one of Whatton's largest jobs was taking away all the merchantable trees on the route of the M1 when it was built, extending from the Bucks. border in the south to Northants. in the north. Thousands of trees came in, many being cut, converted and then sent back for crash-barriers and fence-posts. Up to eight sets of tackle could be seen at one time lined up outside the mill.

The original Latil, that gave over forty years of hard and faithful service, came off the road in 1976 and was put through the firm's workshops and rebuilt by their engineer, Cyril Spriggs, who had cared for and kept the old lady going all her working life. This Latil perhaps won more affection than any other vehicle in the fleet. She was as much at home on the cobbles of London Dockland as in the muddy woods and fields within a radius of forty miles of Hartwell. Most of the drivers had at one time or another over the years had a turn at her wheel. Even Mrs. Agnes Whatton, Eric's wife, drove her when during the war Eric and Archie were at one time taking regular loads of decking up to Liverpool to be shipped to Ireland, a top priority contract, in the thick of air raids and journeys that required a 3 a.m. start. One morning Eric was away with his lorry, but Archie had stalled, become over-choked, and was unable to start. Remembering that his sister-in-law, Agnes, could just about drive the Latil he called her out and she towed him up the road and got him going. Thus the Latil probably became the only one to be driven by a lady in carpet slippers and night attire.

Sadness and bereavement cloud the Whatton story, since Eric's son was tragically killed in a road accident and later Eric's brother, Bob, died. In July 1982, Eric and Archie put away the famous Whatton Slade Mill sign that had stood so long at the front of the mill. The day before had seen the take over of the entire business by its new owners. However, a little bit of Whattons of Hartwell will live on in nearby Bedfordshire, where the Latil now resides still finished in their famous gold livery. When young Eric trudged round with the horse, cart, and faggots, he saw a great future in timber, a dream he was to make a reality in his lifetime. His father's foresight, the tin of coins and the horse all played their part, of course. The Whatton Brothers were no strangers to hard work. They did not have good luck, but they made it, earning well the high respect they came to command in the home-grown timber trade in their time.

*Mr. Whatton senior with the first E.R.F. and a fine Olive Ash*

*The three brothers Whatton, Eric, Bob and Archie*

*The Whatton fleet lines up*

*Eric Whatton loading the E.R.F.*

*A Foden emerges from Althorp Park, Northants with a good elm*

*The Whatton designed trailer and AEC*

# The tram stopper

Before his fourteenth birthday, Denis Brown was helping in his father's timber-haulage business as a trace-horse lad, his job being to wait at the foot of a hill with the horse for a loaded team to arrive, then hook on and, with the added horse, see them up the hill, after which he would either return to the foot for the next team or carry on with the others to repeat the procedure at the next steep incline. At sixteen he was driving a fifteen-ton steam-tractor. He learned his trade early, the hard way.

An advertisement announced, 'Six months guaranteed hauling in Sussex'. William and Denis Brown Hauliers landed the job. It was around 1920 and for a well known timber merchant. The point of the story is that the Brown Brothers were not in Sussex, far from it, they lived and operated around their home town of Darlington in the North, so the long expedition was on to the South. Two complete teams of horses and timber wagons were loaded and put on the rail for Tonbridge Wells via London. The two brothers each drove a steam tractor, a Fowler, and a Ransome with wagon and kit, setting off on the great trek South on the A1. There were no low loaders to hop on to and no motorway to pop down. The 275 mile trip took over a week and went well, that is until they reached Central London, where Denis' engine stopped suddenly without warning. So did the tram car following him, the one after that and so on, and in fact, there were tram cars as far back as he could see, with an ever increasing crowd of irate tram-drivers, conductors, inspectors and police gathered around, all with the same message, "You can't possibly stop here in the middle of the tram-way". Not only that, it was Derby Day, too. By now the trouble was evident, the winch rope had jumped over the drum and was firmly matted in the drive sprocket, hence the sudden stop. Can you imagine the amount of jacking, blocking up, barring, hammering and chiselling required to remove the fouling rope. Well they had just got the wheel off, when the top brass from the tramway's department pushed through the crowd and added his twopennyworth of protest to the Brown brothers. Denis explained, in a few well-chosen words which I will not repeat, how he had not come all the way down from the North with the view of stopping trams. After all, he and his brother were being somewhat inconvenienced as well. Not only that, he said that if the interference ceased, work to free the steaming engine could continue. Free it they did and soon the Brown cavalcade and most of London's trams rolled again. The horses were unloaded and driven across London and the sight of all four sets of tackle crossing London Bridge was one to be long remembered by many astonished Londoners.

Well, they made it and Brown Brothers whose slogan was 'Enterprise and slogging hard work with integrity', completed the job. They came to work for six months, but stayed hauling for Turner's Sawmills for thirty years. Before that, though, Denis Brown launched out on his own account, operating from Billbrook in the Midlands. Soon the early Latils, of which he had five over the years, and then several Unipowers and Foden Artics, all featured in his fleet. He finally settled at Woodchester near Stroud, Gloucester, where he became main haulier to Henry Workman's Sawmills.

When many were interviewed for this book they were proud to be the first ever to do this or that in this industry. Denis Brown had been not only the first to perform some hitherto believed impossible task, but occasionally the only one.

Showing a photograph of a fine load of oak running back over fifty feet long behind a Unipower, he said, "I took that load from Chester to Warrington through the Mersey Tunnel". "Did that length exceed the regulations?" I asked, to which he replied, "Half the time, the tails were rubbing the walls, but if timber merchants don't want them cutting you have to bend the rules. Trees never grow in accordance with the traffic act".

A timber merchant summoned Denis over to Wales. The Llangollen Canal had burst its banks and undermined the railway. A locomotive had overturned and rolled down the bank just out of reach of a huge railway steam crane. The problem was pulling the loco. thirty yards to the reach of the crane. The army turned up with some of the biggest snatch blocks Denis had ever seen. They virtually had to drag them into place. Setting up was the biggest part. It all depended on the block and rope set-up. They were working to a calculation of over a sixty-ton line pull. Very slowly the ropes took the tension from block to block, then from loco to tractor. Denis put the Unipower in bottom gear and gave her a little throttle leaving the rest to her makers Messrs. Universal Power Drives and Gardner Engines. The ropes now were barely moving as the anchor dug in and settled down to the pull of a lifetime, with faith pinned in the snatch blocks and elaborate rope set-up. Literally, inch by inch, the giant load edged towards the hook of the crane and once more the locomotive was back on the rails. An engineer from Unipowers once told me about the first time he had seen one of his machines pulling a tree. He had no idea of the rigours of timbering and said that his heart missed several beats. What a good job he was not with Denis Brown that day in Wales! He would have had a full-blown coronary.

Denis favoured the Crane Four-in-Line fifteen-ton trailers. Their legal weight limit was higher than his Tandem axle-configuration. Three bookings for over-loading had taught him this.

Today, the fleet of Denis Brown and Son (Peter) consists of an ERF (Cummins) Unit, a Leyland Road Train, three Matadors, a Caterpillar 955 and 'Big Alice', an Allis Chalmers Loader that will pick up 275 cubic feet in one bite. Peter and employee Ron operate from Cornwall to Norfolk and throughout the Midlands. In keeping with tradition they carry some rare loads. Peter's two beautifully restored Standard cars (circa 1920) are the family's pride and joy, as will be the pre-war Latil he is working on.

It is my practice when interviewing eighty-year-old-plus characters to consider their expected frailties in order not to over excite or tire them. In this frame of mind, I visited Denis Brown. How wrong I was! It was I who was left tired and exhausted. Denis was in the workshop with Peter who was heating an obstinate pin and it was Denis on the hammer knocking merry hell out of the same. Finally, I came near to upsetting him by discussing retirement. Rephrasing my words, I asked "When did you actually come off the road?" "I haven't yet", came the sharp reply. "I drove up to Lincoln last week and this afternoon I'm going twenty miles to buy some timber".

At this point Peter added that dad had recently, when short-handed, driven a Crawler pulling out timber. "I enjoy work. I enjoy life", were Denis's parting words. So how do we remember Denis Brown, the man who drove a Fowler from North to South, the haulier who held up more trams than the rest of us put together, the man who at eighty-two and a half years old could and would, if required, still go and put a load of timber on? We must remember him by all of these things. But our timber haulage industry was pioneered by men who toiled unceasingly with trees that often presented a near unanswerable task. Some of those men are featured in this book, men who climbed the ladders of this dangerous profession from the first rung to the top and Denis Brown is one of them.

The William and Denis Brown Story is not complete without mention of their nephew, David, who started his working life driving Fordson Tractors fitted with Cooke winches, and then progressed to Unipowers. Designing timber tractors rather than driving them was to be where his future lay. At Muir-Hill Tractors, he designed and manufactured eight-wheel-drive logging tractors fitted with cranes for the Scandinavian market.

Today, D. J. B. Brown heads D. J. B. Engineering Ltd. in Peterlee, County Durham. Besides designing and manufacturing underground mining tractors, giant dump trucks and other earth-moving equipment, they build and export a massive 4 × 4 timber tractor and pole trailer designed to carry pay loads of over 2000 cubic feet (50 to 60 metric tons, 80 tons on the larger 6 × 6 model) powered by world-famous Caterpillar engines of 460 F.W. HP.

In the Cameroons they are covering 100-150 mile round-trips, over bush roads and through swamps in conditions bordering on the impossible for man and machine. Eighty years of Brown timber haulage experience has gone into these giants. David Brown tells me one of these gigantic wheels cost more than half as much again of the purchase price of his first Fordson Major.

He did not tell me, however, that his Company has been awarded three Queen's Awards, two for export achievement in 1978 and 1981 and one in 1980 for technological achievement. The company also gained the Design Council Award for outstanding British products. William Brown's secret was enterprise, integrity and slogging hard work, all attributes that would appear to be hereditary.

*Denis at the wheel of the first Latil*

*A post war Latil with four in line trailer*

*Hannibals on parade*

*Peter's Artics 1984*

*The giant Allis Charmer "Big Alice"*

*A tight squeeze (note the men cross-cutting)*

*A D.J.B. outfit at work in the Cameroons (no motorway contraflows for this chap)*

*BVF 471 Her first day out*

# Prime oak

When major restoration work was required at St. Margaret's, Piccadilly, London, the architects specified not only prime oak, but the finest obtainable in the land. Their choice was Norfolk-grown timbers from the estate of the Duke of Grafton, bought, felled, hauled and milled by Messrs. Coughtrey of Griston, near Thetford. In April, 1982, Mr. Fred Coughtrey paused from work in the garden of his bungalow, where he now enjoys retirement from the old sawmill next door, which for many years was his life. Pointing to the built up area over the road, he said, "Before the development that was a seventeen-acre field where my grandfather grazed the teams of horses that brought the first timber to his Griston Mill back in the 1800s." The giant oil engine, still there, superseded the pitsaws. Fred recalls one gifted old sawyer who, day in and day out, would regularly cut boards seven eights of an inch thick precisely with the eight foot long one-way pitsaw, board after board, without the slightest fluctuation.

After driving steam tackle for eleven years, Mr. Coughtrey's father bought a brand new Latil and four-wheel drug, plus a second-hand vehicle. The picture shows the first load coming into Griston. Fred was full of nothing but praise for the bright red Latil and the big loads the little petrol engine pulled, right up to the day of his retirement. One memorable occasion was when Fred arrived at the railway station with a four hundred-plus cubic foot elm and was all set to roll it on to the bolster wagon concerned. This he could have done in moments. However, the old station master insisted that the tree should be dropped to the ground and as regulations required, two giant cranes should be brought up all the way from Ipswich especially to load it. Fred's comment was, 'Railway rules are railway rules'.

The firm though small had a great name for quality oak and in their day had exported it to New Zealand. A Cambridge based firm of architects frequently brought their own craftsmen to select a choice butt in the yard. One such occasion was when a superb, clean, long butt was chosen and hewn into a splendid spiral pillar now standing in St. Paul's Cathedral. If you ever go there, admire the skill and craft of the men who shaped it by all means, but spare a thought for the fallers who felled it without a split or shake, for the little red Latil, and for Fred Coughtrey who safely hauled it home.

*The Latils first Oak into Griston*

*A prime oak*

*Penrith (1922)*

# The enterprising church warden

Back in 1870, the vicar of Silsden in Yorkshire became anxious about two large dangerous elm trees in the churchyard so he asked his church warden, Jeremiah Green, the local coal-merchant, to arrange to have them felled. In doing so, he had unknowingly sown the seed that was to grow into one of the best known timber companies of its day — Arthur Green of Silsden Ltd. It seems that those two elm trees set Jeremiah thinking, so much so that he closed his coal business and started buying trees. His son, Arthur, took over in 1899 when Jeremiah died and his other son, John, joined the company for a time leaving later to trade separately. Jeremiah's grandson, Jerry, joined the company in 1935 until 1975 when his sons, Richard and Andrew took over. Andrew continues to run the company and Richard now runs a Continental haulage company.

In researching for this book I have found that the name of Arthur Green of Silsden has cropped up all over the country. A lady in Suffolk remembered that as a girl, Greens were working in her village. The men gave the children rides to school on the horses and the children cried when one horse was injured and had to be put down. I heard of a job in Wales where the trees were growing on an almost inaccessible site and were sold two or three times because no one could extract them until a firm from Yorkshire came — They got them out all right.

In their heyday, Arthur Green's had twenty-eight lorries, including subcontractors, one hundred and fifty woodfallers, and thirty woodleaders with tractors pulling out and loading. They used to move over one million cubic feet of timber a year operating from Scotland to the Home Counties and from Norfolk to Wales. There, they introduced their famous three legs for loading. 'Buyers of Standing Timber in Any Part of the Country for Cash' ran their well known advertisement. They used teams of horses with one white horse in each team up to 1944, but bought their first motor lorry, a Leyland Badger, in 1934. Their practice was to dispatch the horses and wagons by rail to the distant jobs, where generally the trees were then hauled into the nearby station.

It is interesting to note that the Company never used steam or road tractors and carriages, but went from horses direct to artics. Apart from one or two ERFs and Commers they very much favoured Leylands right from 1934 to 1969 when they changed to Scanias. The traditional pole trailer was changed to a trailer with six bolsters so that shorter lengths of timber could be carried legally.

The humble duties of Church Warden seldom lead to a nationally known and highly respected timber concern, but for the Greens of Silsden they did.

35

*952 cu. ft. spruce,*
*Dumfries, Scotland.*
*Now that is a load*

*1922 Great Ouseburn*
*North Yorkshire*

*One of the Scanias*

*Fir trees from Coombes Wood,*
*Armathwhite, Cumbria*

36

# Women in a timberman's world

In looking for material for this book, one fact became increasingly obvious, and that is the part ladies have played in timber production, particularly during the last war. I either met or heard of women who carried out every operation including chain-sawing, saw-doctoring and operating band mills. One had served second person in a lopping team and worked irregularly as mate on a timber tractor for several years. Another completely managed and organised a timber haulage business of many vehicles.

Edith Darke chuckled about her first memories of wood. During the hour off from school, she and her brothers had to deliver firewood loaded in handcarts. With the cart guided down the hill by the tram lines that passed the yard, they would speed down the dip, in spite of the trams. That was fun.

At thirteen, life was far from fun. She left school and became a waggoner's mate with one of her father's two timber carting teams. This involved being called at five o'clock in the morning, fetching the thirteen horses from across the town with her brother, grooming and feeding them, putting a bit of candle in the waggon's back lamp, and setting off at six with a four-horse team under the care of a seventy-one year old waggoner named Jack. She trudged fourteen miles to Elmley Castle, loaded trees and returned again in the dark regularly, three days a week. The other three days were used for short local hauls. They were hauling oak which her two uncles pit-sawed into baulks for canal lock-gates. On her fourteenth birthday, Jack allowed her to load her first tree unaided. They were hauling trees into Evesham Station at that time.

One day, they overtook a lad in charge of a jibbing horse, that would not even try to pull. Edith helped out by hooking on a trace horse and pulling him up the hill. Two years later, by coincidence, she met the lad again when she was hauling from his father's farm. They courted for seven years and then married — all thanks to the 'jibbing horse'.

Edith learned all the tricks of the trade. Her own horses sometimes hesitated in the woods knowing they would be aided by the use of pulley blocks if the job got too bad. Discovering this, she would unhook the horses, rattle the blocks, and refasten the traces. Then the team would pull away with confidence as if the blocks were in use.

Her brother, Len, carried scars on his face from the kick of a vicious horse that would also lay back its ears and bite. They sometimes used this energy by getting a small lad to run just in front of the horse egging him on. One horse that had come out of the army was a good worker, but always lay down when they stopped. This was disastrous at times. Edith remembers often dreading that this might happen if the bobby should stop them as they came up Broad Street in Worcester with a load. The policeman was informed of this, however, and generally waved them on.

She recollected how the frozen chains would skin her hands in the hard winters. When the steamers came, the farmers refused to have the big ironed-wheels in the field so the horses and Edith were kept on for loading. Of the Darke steamers she remembers 'Starlight' and 'Busy Bee', but favoured a fast little engine named, 'I can

Hoppit'. With a chuckle and with a twinkle in her eye she confessed, 'I drove that engine through Worcester many a time'.

At seventeen, she came off hauling and concentrated on the farm where she milked and mucked out. She mostly drove a big dray, carting feed stuff and doing general haulage, and was ticked off on one occasion for driving too fast. Darke's had three blacksmiths and two wheelwrights. Edith did her share of shoeing mules and donkeys for the canal people during World War 1. Even today, she can describe in detail the wheelwright's art of fitting steel tyres, as she remembers every aspect of timber in those times.

At eighty she is fit, bright and spritely. 'A most wonderful old lady' were Ben Hinton's words and it is to him we are thankful for finding her and going to see her, even after the story of S. Darke and Sons had been written.

During the last war, a forestry section of the Women's Land Army became, in 1942, the Women's Timber Corps with five thousand, five hundred members throughout the British Isles. Bette Anderson was a Lumber Jill, as they were nicknamed. She told me the girls trained and became tractor drivers, (wheeled and crawler), lorry drivers, looked after and handled trace-horses tushing out, and felled and cross-cut all sorts of timber. They drove massive sawmill cranes, light railway locomotives, barges on the canals, and even carried out log rafting on the Scottish Lochs. Their hard work and efficiency eventually overcame suspicions harboured by some men. Bette remembered one petite lass about five feet tall, who, in spite of her dainty appearance, could handle a crawler with great dexterity. Chips Wood, as they called her, was sent to replace a sick man in a haulage gang who, with their bonus in mind, at first refused point-blank to take this mere pint-sized wisp of a girl, but had no choice. With every eye on her, Chips soon got the feel of the huge crawler and then started work. Could she handle that big Cat! She made it sit up and beg. Later, a request was made to keep her full-time in the gang.

Bette recalled being in a lorry gang taking poles to an airfield. Security was tight, but clearance was given at the guard-room, where the airmen fell over themselves to do escort duty for this lorry load of bronzed beauties. Somehow, after unloading, they took a wrong turning and found they were lost. The gate-guard had changed and they were, in fact, present without authority. Again a horde of airmen regaled them with refreshment whilst a release permit was found. However, the girls got the impression that no one was trying very hard. After this, all-girl-gangs were not sent to airfields again from this forestry unit.

I wonder how many of you remember the first Darnarm two-man chain-saw. Bette was in the Forest of Dean when the prototype was being tested and she and a well-built friend were invited to be photographed using it. The idea was to handle this heavy brute with nonchalant ease and girlish grace, the theme being 'light and safe enough for a woman to handle'. Actually, it nearly pulverised them. They claimed their arms never did return to their original length.

The exploits of Amy Parsons and Rosemary Hucker have been taken from the Henry Giles story. In this way, the ladies, who have toiled in timber, have the chapter of their own that they deserve. I was not privileged to meet Amy Parsons, but a woman who could administer such a large fleet of timber haulage vehicles and crawlers throughout the war, plus all the extra paper work of the three Ministry of Supply vehicles on loan, and who took a Unipower out to a job, when no one else was on hand, must have been quite a lady. Today, we have come to accept very successful women in all walks of business yet even as Mrs. Hucker talked of the capacities of

38

vehicles such as the Matador, Militant and Mandator, I knew these were not just three M's that cropped up in her files, but rather vehicles whose abilities she understood perfectly and on whose cabs was carried the name of Henry Giles.

Henry Giles has always been a family firm. When the second world war started, the administration of such items as petrol coupons was essential to survival, but Henry was no administrator. It was his daughter Amy, Mrs. Parsons, who took control. Henry managed the work, but Amy managed the office and, as far as she could, the money. It was not easy to stop her father spending the income before it came in. It was through Mrs. Parsons that the business was established on a more secure footing and became more efficiently organised.

Henry died in 1956 and it was daughter, Amy, and his younger son, Stanley, who took over the business, continuing to trade in the name of Henry Giles, but that partnership was brought to a tragic end in 1964, when Stanley was killed, aged 47. A tree fell on him whilst he was unloading a pole-carriage in a timber yard. Mrs. Parsons took over the business as the sole proprietor. She must have been the first woman ever to run a firm of timber contractors, but she had a quarter of century's experience behind her. Her first major problem arose when she was given notice to quit the yard in Bath where the firm had been established for years, and that at a time when she was still struggling with the settlement due for brother Stanley's death. Her daughter, Rosemary, and her son-in-law bought an old sawmill near Frome and the business moved there in 1967. Her other major problem was her own health, since she was dogged by a heart condition. She reduced the size of the business considerably to make it manageable within her own limitations, but died following a heart operation in November, 1970. Her daughter, Rosemary Hucker, took over. She had been close to her grandfather as a child, riding all the horses he would buy, giving him much pleasure.

Mrs. Hucker took over the business when road-haulage legislation was on the increase. Improved standards were required for road safety. She had to cope with MOT tests for tractor units and trailers alike. She had to organise the work within the limitations of drivers' hours and weight restrictions. She had to satisfy the requirements of an Operator's Licence and an Operating Centre. Conditions of employment had also become more complicated. It was such a different world from the one her grandfather knew. Her cousin Roger worked for her from time to time, but she was the one keeping Henry Giles alive. Like her mother before her, she found that her business dealings were always with men. She was no stranger to fetching and carrying parts, taking spare-wheels for breakdowns on motorways, and taking a turn at the wheel, as at the time when the Bray loader needed pulling out of a drain hole, or when a load of timber needed roping out of a wood. I was fascinated to read a project her son, Martin, wrote at the age of ten at school entitled "A History of Timber Haulage". He had covered every aspect from flint axe-heads for felling to a comprehensive explanation of the fifth-wheel-coupling and modern hydraulic loaders. It was marvellous.

Timber contracting was never easy. Not many families have shown such resolution to maintain a name, and it was the girls who were the mainstay. In the end it was the recession of 1980 which beat them and Mrs. Hucker ceased trading. If the end had not come then, it would probably have had to come later when the men, trained by Henry in the work he knew so well, retired. It was the experience of these men that was the real wealth of the business, and those who took a turn at managing the firm worked closely with them.

As the men were called up, the home timber trade became more and more dependent on the women of our land. Without their efforts, the war could have dragged on. Doubtless our Lumber Jills saved the day as have other ladies who have toiled in timber since.

*Women's Timber Corps in the 1st World War at Ludlow*

*Women's Timber Corps in the 2nd World War — a bevy of beauties in Devon*
Reproduced by kind permission of Mrs. Dora Oliver

# The Champion Oak

In 1939, a severe gale blew down the 'Champion Oak', as it was known, that had stood for eight hundred years in the deer park at Powis Castle, Welshpool, and which was accepted at that time to be the largest oak tree in Great Britain. The three main limbs yielded one thousand cubic feet of beautiful timber. The trunk being twenty feet in length by twenty four feet in circumference was just too big. No sawmill was large enough to take it, so it lay in the park for ten years until in 1949 Jabez Barker Ltd., timber merchants of Shrewsbury, came along and bought the massive tree. Their facilities for transportation or milling were no different from those of others, but their insight and acumen for business were. They brought in a highly-skilled explosive expert from Macclesfield, who studied the proposition with great care and then completely split the tree with three charges. The damage was so small that the huge trunk itself rendered a further one thousand cubic feet of perfectly sound timber.

This sets the scene for yet another account of a most successful company. Grandson, George, and great-grandson, Robert Barker, showed a large press and photograph album to my friend, Ben Hinton. Jabez Barker founded the firm in 1874. George recalled that he had a unit of seven four-horse teams and how he would dispatch corn and feed by rail to jobs right across Shropshire, Herefordshire and Wales, where they worked in every parish in Montgomeryshire. A gang of ten fellers covered a vast acreage. In Anglesey, they worked for over a year felling one hundred and fifty thousand cubic feet, often using only axes, producing top quality ash and sycamore timbers. It was company policy to buy up entire estates, large mansion houses, farms, cottages, the lot. After felling the merchantable timber, they would replant and then resell. At one time the firm had four such estates in its hands.

First horses, then one Burrell and two Foster Steam Tractors, hauled into local railway stations, where Barker's installed their own cranes for such was the volume of timber. The biggest load ever put on a railway truck was the one thousand, one hundred and fifty cubic feet of Douglas fir in 1932. In 1934, the purchase of a new Caterpillar Model 50 with Hyster Double Drum Winch was a sensation and featured in Caterpillar sales leaflets. Later Caterpillars D4, 6, 7 and 8 plus a TD14 tractor were used in tushing out on vast jobs now appearing. As steam gave way to diesel, the chain drive TG5 Foden came, the first of many Fodens, a name that became a favourite. Later four STG 5's, one STG6 and 6 × 4 tractor (JUX 135, still preserved today) made up the team of their vehicles which included Latil, Unipower and four Douglas tractors plus two ex-WD six-wheeled Matadors. Robert Barker remembered buying the Matadors for £200 each and converting them. Artic units were made up of tractors by Dodge, AEC, Mandators and a Mammoth. The larger jobs were planned to run three sets of tackle together and loading was with a logging jib. The vehicles were well turned out in the firm's own livery, which is also seen on Robert Barker's pride and joy, an immaculate Matador that he enjoys rallying.

Jabez Barker Ltd., grew to become one of the most successful companies in timber, as perhaps one should expect from the men who found a way of converting a big useless tree into so much fine timber, an idea it seems that had evaded all others in ten long years.

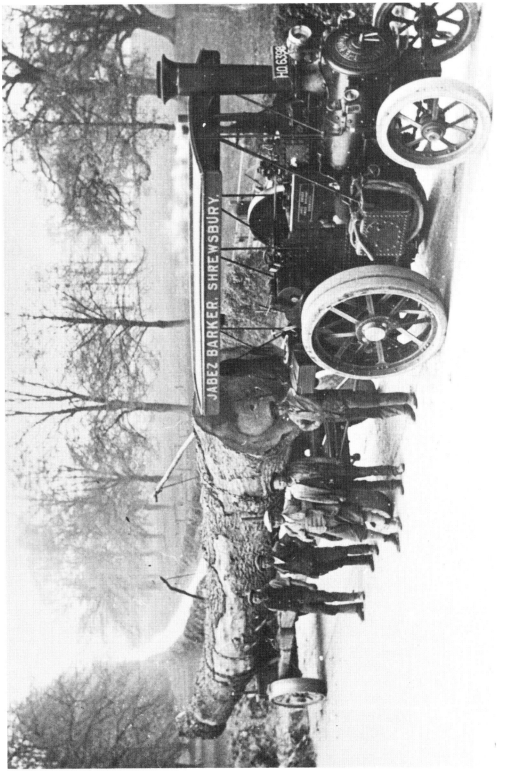

*Oak from Powis Castle Estate (late 1920's)*

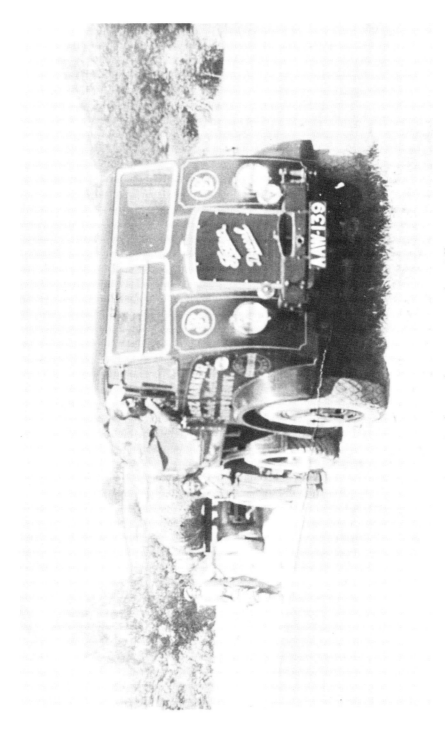

*A nice Foden and a pretty Lumber-Jill*

43

*One of the four STG 5 Fodens*

*The new Hyster double drum winch 1934*

*1,150 cube of Douglas Fir on one waggon. Note Barker's own
crane jib*

*The Chain Drive Foden unloading in Penygroes railway yard*

*An AEC mammoth load*

*Taskers can take it!*

45

*A helping hand on Porlock Hill*

46

# Unipower

After much searching, I finally tracked down Tim Powell. He was the only link left with the old company, Universal Power Drives Ltd., founded back in 1933 by his father, Tom Powell, who had teamed up with Hans Rzeppa, a brilliant young Austrian engineer, who had perfected the famous Rzeppa Constant Velocity Joint, used among other things in war-time in Admiralty power boats.

We could be forgiven for thinking that the Unipower's well known double-drive and trailing axle and chassis extension, plus forestry tractors were all they made. Far from it, for it is interesting to note other productions included front-wheel-drive cars and rear-engined cars, aircraft refuelling bowsers, aircraft tugs, 4 × 4 open-cast coal shovels, War Department gun tractors, logging arches and timber drugs. The export market for specialist oil-field equipment, Unipower junior tractors, Hannibals and later the Invader, was tremendous. In 1956, the introduction of the Centipede, four-wheel drive and steering, to compete with the Latil never really had a chance to succeed. However, the company gained and held a sizeable share of the timber-tractor market.

Tim Powell held various positions in the company and in the oil industry. His famous grandfather was Francis Edward Powell, an American citizen who played a very important part in the fostering of Anglo-American friendship which was so vital during the two World Wars, and who was instrumental in forming the Anglo-American Oil Co., of which he was President for many years, and which has now developed into the Esso Petroleum Co. Ltd. Regrettably, Tom Powell died in 1971 at the age of 64 years. In spite of failing health, he was actively engaged in vehicle design until the end.

Forty years or more on, there are many Unipower tractors still around, several completely restored and kept for rallying, whilst quite a few are still at work, as is my own. Managing Director, Peter Rotheroe, told me that Unipower Vehicles Ltd., live on and continue to manufacture very high power weight ratio (400/500 bhp) for four or six-wheel drive vehicles for military and emergency applications — making as ever a specialist, high quality product. Gigantic vehicles are being made now. They are perhaps beyond the comprehension of most people, but are all in a direct line of descent from those Foresters and Hannibals that carved the name of Unipower in wood and kept it there for thirty or more years.

*Three in a row*

*The Unipower Junior (Export)*                                              *Rising to the occasion. Field trials*

*A typical loading scene*

*The Unipower Executive and others*

# Tom Pain

"I want you in hospital immediately". It was a command, not a friendly invitation, that was being made by a senior specialist to Tom H. Pain of Cleobury Mortimer, near Kidderminster, Worcestershire. The reply was almost automatic. There was no way he could go in at that time. All his hard work in business was now starting to bear fruit. With a hundred on the pay roll and at the height of his career, with many irons in the fires of commerce, it was quite out of the question and Tom bluntly said so.

As a lad, a farmer's son, Tom had hankered after engines and machines. In his early teens he landed a partnership with a much older man who had threshing tackle and moved a bit of timber. Tom's first steam tractor, a fine little Garrett engine is featured here with iron-wheeled-pole-wagon and a tidy stick upon it. "I drove that little engine hundreds of miles", Tom recalled with pleasure. In 1928 he bought a solid-tyred Fordson Tractor. If not so powerful, it was found to be more versatile, wanted no firing and kept him a lot cleaner.

If there is one thread that weaves through Tom Pain's life it is the one of always being ready to modify and improve anything that can be made to give either better, longer, easier or safer service. There was one thing spoilt a good winch that Tom owned. It wasn't intended for an anchor. Tom designed one and asked the winch makers to make it for him. However, they were not impressed at first, but then on second thoughts made it and happily many more to sell to others. Later on, other inventions included the development of a turn-table locking pin that fitted at the end of the swan neck on the pole of his ERF trailers thus enabling one man to disconnect the unit with ease in minutes. His fitting of a winch on an ERF Artic making it a self-loader via pulleys was a success, but never really caught on with the drivers.

With the advent of the Latil, like many others, Tom was right in at the start and soon became the owner of two new tractors. The photograph shows them with a large oak butt on each trailer, approximately 350 cubic feet in each. Note their size beside the man standing on the draw bar. Tom had nothing but praise for his Latils even though his huge loads on the steep hills around Cleobury burnt out many a valve from high revving in low gear. Eventually, he approached Perkins who came up with the P6 for him, the first to go into a Latil. An engineer lived with him for ten days to tune it to perfection and it must have been time well spent in view of all the Perkins engines to be fitted in Latils later on.

For ages, Fodens had courted Tom and tried hard to sell him a steamer, but all without success. Then one day, they wrote asking him if he would come up to Sandbach where they were making, for the first time, two chain-drive diesel tractors with transverse Gardner 5LW engines. They said that if he would buy one at a nominal price, for two years they would modify, update and repair it at their expense and at the end of that period rebuild the tractor back to its original condition. A deal was struck and Tom had the first tractor. The other went to Coltman's of Rugby under the same arrangement.

Foden's engineers often worked through the night and weekends and were always available for development problems. The winch had an inch cable and the orders were, 'Show the tractor no mercy'. The machine came out of it all extremely well and Tom laid great emphasis on the fact that as always, "Fodens kept their agreement to the letter", so it's not surprising an order was later made for a shaft-drive tractor for which was specified a 6LW engine. This was yet another favourite tractor in the fleet, which was also to include several Fordson Tractors. Some of these were tested for Fords and Tom also tested cross-country tyres for Dunlop's. His fleet also included a Unipower, ERFs and finally several Matadors which he used to haul all over Herefordshire, Gloucestershire, Wales and even in Scotland when once asked to send tackle up there. During the war, Tom also had an agricultural implement business and became the local Ford Dealer. The first twelve tractors were sold as fast as he could get them. Tom recalled unpacking the first combine harvester in the district, which came boxed up from Canada. Price — £750.

Tom Pain saw work as something to be done and he thrived on it. He was never happier than when engaged in one of his enterprises which at one time included running the local cinema. Yet, in spite of all this, he still made time for work in public life. Note, however, that he was the first to admit dependence on his wife and the fine team of people who rather worked with him than for him. For this he expected to pay above the going rate. The value of such back-up, for example, was with his engineer, who could weld and fit second to none. He was a man who would work through the night on a Latil's big end and have it rolling for 7.30 next morning. When he attended a seized Fordson tractor in the field, he removed the engine on the spot, returning with a service replacement unit on site. When their Caterpillar D6 was working without a sump-guard, a jagged rock ripped the sump extensively, but they didn't fetch it home. The driver was asked to dig a hole as deeply as possible between the tracks. The engineer returned, produced a sheet of copper plate and skilfully beat, moulded, drilled, tapped and fitted it. No temporary job this, it lasted years. In the very early days with Latil, Tom had occasion to ring the London works for a small gear-box part whereupon they nearly had a fit. "No engineer unless trained by us could possibly carry out the task", said the voice at the other end, but Tom insisted, "Put it on the half-past one train for Worcester. We'll come back to you if we are stuck." Needless to say, they weren't.

Now let us return to that fateful day in 1949. The specialist was right. Tom faced four major operations and three years of semi-invalidity. Unknowingly, Tom had prepared for this time in the building of staff relationships so his business did not go to the wall. His wife took over the overall running and every worker his own side of the business. Friends rallied round, but best of all, Tom's biggest customer, who depended on the timber from Pain's Sawmill, to keep them going, undertook to buy the trees they wanted for Tom on his behalf, a situation that demanded the greatest possible trust and it all worked out. Tom survived this grim time in his life because of his wise investment of goodwill which paid him high dividends in his adversity.

In June 1983, Tom is retired. He loves to work in his large garden, that gives him much pleasure. He still has many irons in the fire. The drive that once went into commerce is redirected now into public life, where he serves unceasingly, his particular niche being youth education, for he has always fervently believed any boy or girl who has the slightest inclination to get on should be helped as much as possible. His time with school governors and on committees has done much to bring this about. Although unaware of it, many young persons owe their chance in life to Tom H. Pain of Cleobury Mortimer, the man of many talents who loved engines and tractors and loved making them work better for everyone.

*Kinlet Estate: preparing to load*

*Will these skids take 350 cube?*

*A couple of valve burning loads!*

51

*The first Foden Diesel*

*Coltman's Foden in the mud (note rear wheel cleats)*

*Tom's Garrett*

52

# Bernard and Jim

The brothers Bernard and Jim Davies of Bucknell, Salop, could have expected a fine inheritance from the sawmill their father had so successfully built up during the first World War. It was founded around 1860 by their grandfather, a local blacksmith. I say "could have" but the slump of the 1920's almost ruined their father. Therefore, they started from scratch with joint talents, Bernard in the timber trade and Jim as an engineer, who cared for all the machinery in both the mill and the field. Together they worked hard and built a concern known and highly respected throughout the timber trade today.

Bernard's son, Peter, has a giant photograph album which really says it all. His grandfather was a boxing enthusiast as was his friend, the local squire. Quite often when a price for a parcel of timber could not be agreed between them, they would box for the outstanding amount in a gymnasium built in the garage. A snapshot taken in 1922 shows two of the many Davies steam tractors loading a giant butt that cubed at 700 feet. One beloved steamer named 'Old Martha' featured much over the years. Later several Latils and three Unipowers served, but the name of Foden topped the lot by far. At one time, over three hundred were employed at the five and a half acre yard, which was a major source of work in Bucknall involving several families including a father and six sons. In their heyday, some seventy vehicles counting tractors, lorries and vans were registered. The firm had its own workshops, painters, signwriters and coachbuilders who produced an exclusive ash-framed cab. Note the unique canopy hood over the cab back, reminiscent of the early Latils. Of an old ex-WD Scammel, I asked Peter "Was she not too cumbersome or slow?" "Yes", he agreed, but added, "When a winching job was really tough that old lady would just stand there and pull and pull". As for Foden, they had 6 × 4 artic and winch tractors, bolster wagons, ERFs, ex-WD G.M.C. 6 × 6 tractors and even Bren gun carriers.

In the 1950s, the Rolls-Royce turbo-blown engined Vickers VR180 huge crawler tractor, coupled mostly to the giant Onions Sulky spent two years in Bernard and Jim's hands, being developed and driven often round the clock on some of their worst sites. With a fifteen mph speed, the return travel time when tushing out was often doubled. The first Davies Crawler was an International in 1931. However, I note Peter Davies spoke most highly of the timber man's old favourite, the Fowler Challenger Three, with tracks and a Leyland 600 engine. It seemed to run for ever. They also ran several Cats, D6 and D7s and even an ex-WD armoured D6. Jim Davies designed and built much equipment, one of his successes being the cutting off of the back end of an ex-WD Crossley and grafting it to a LeTourneau USA crane. The re-engined Gardner 4LW unit drove on the front wheels whilst the rear prop-shaft drove the crane winch. This high jib, lowered for travelling, would lift eight to ten tons making it a super loader. One of their more difficult jobs was in the Tintern Forest, Chepstow, where some magnificent timber had grown on a nigh inaccessible position, entry to which was along a narrow ledge just wide enough to take a vehicle. Since the trees were large and not to be tushed they had no option but to go in with two crane units hoisting the trunks, one each end, then carrying them out over a mile with one crane reversing all the way. The Davies family worked closely with Morland Matches (England's Glory) supplying them with prime poplar for match making. In return they took all Morland surplus poplar not suitable for their requirements. The

Queen of the Fleet is a T registered AEC Militant 6 × 6 with three line braking. An International engine powers the Highland Bear Loader, model 1500, the largest mobile they make, a magnificent vehicle designed by the Davies Company and a glutton for work, picking up 5 to 6 tons and up to 1¾ tons at full reach.

Bernard Davies was appalled at the terrible war-time over-cutting of our woodlands and laid down a tree nursery commencing a large planting programme. It became his greatest interest and the rehabilitation of the Welsh border woodland owes much to him, a fact that came from his obituary written by Mr. Charles Venables, O.B.E. in 1977. He also wrote of the brothers, "He and his brother Jim expanded to become one of the largest distributors of round native logs in the U.K." During the Second War, the business expanded still further, with no prospect of personal gain, due to excess profits tax, but with the determination to play a vigorous part in the war effort. As I was serving with the Home Timber Production Department, I saw a lot of Bernard. He could always be relied on to send a load of oak logs to some city mill very short of raw material, or a load of boatskin larch to some boatbuilder anxious to complete one of the small craft vital to the Royal Navy. In this he was ably supported by his brother, who kept the large fleet of road vehicles and extraction equipment in first class order, even though it was all being grossly overworked.

Today, Peter Davies has two sons who are both away, one studying forestry, the other forest-tree nursery craft. Bernard and Jim Davies of Bucknall have moved their share of trees, but their efforts in woodland regeneration will delight many a conservationist and future tree lovers for decades to come.

*Approx 28 tons in one lump*

*Loading 700 cube in 1922*

*A nice 6 wheeled Foden*

*The faithful old Scammell*

*One of the Davies built cabs. Note Latil type canopy*

*The first Latil early 1930*

*The Crossley Crane Jim Davies built*

*One of the many Fodens*

*The AEC Militant 6 × 6 1984*

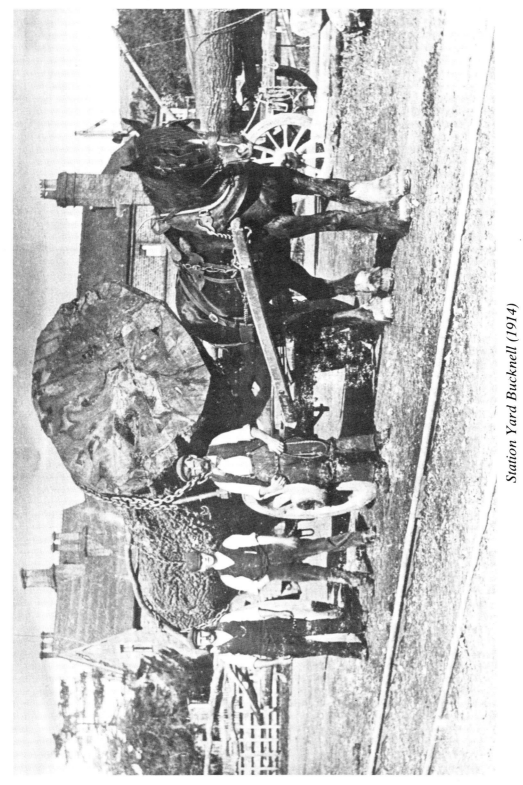

*Station Yard Bucknell (1914)*

57

*Marshall Engine at Craven Arm during World War I*

*Fowler Engine hauling oak into Bucknell (1920)*

*Jackknife at Bridgenorth, Fowler hauling 3 trailers to Birmingham (1922)*

*Old Martha Marshall with 3 trailers*

*Foden hauling elm from Ludlow (1928)*

62

# Moving one of God's Giants

'F. Scarsbrook and Sons Ltd., Woodstock', was a name cleverly painted across the rear bolster of their Tasker pole trailer. You may have seen it around Oxfordshire. Fred Scarsbrook was a saddler, but the falling work-horse population caused him to turn to the coal trade. However, it was the coal famine of 1926 that brought him to timber when he would buy tree tops, axe out the cord wood, and saw logs with a Lister-driven engine. He worked hard to build a future for his growing family, eventually, three sons Arthur, Nigel, Jack and daughters Cynthia and Lilian. It was Cynthia and Jack who gave me the story and loaned me the photographs.

Starting with two horse teams, Fred hauled around and on the nearby Blenheim Palace estate and woodlands. The first tractor was an early Fordson. A treasured photograph depicts a tidy lime tree secured or twitched by what they called 'wickering sticks'. Later, an Auto-Mower winch, which they liked, was fitted to this tractor, as was a later Fordson which I saw pictured hauling one of the early diseased elms at Blenheim as far back as 1938.

Jack Scarsbrook undertook much of the engineering and built a superb timber carriage. Land clearance for the wartime aerodromes featured with a Wallis Stevens ploughing engine, named 'The March Hare', used for root grubbing. Later, this engine gave valiant service in the mill driving the machinery.

Perhaps the most interesting vehicle was the FWD, re-engined with a Gardner and painted beautifully in red. It was prepared for Nigel to take over when he came out of the army. They also operated an AEC Matador which like the FWD, which I've heard elsewhere, was always kept immaculate. Fred Scarsbrook found time for work in public life serving on the Woodstock Council where he once topped the polls. He loved sport as did his sons.

In the early 1920s, Canavon Partners Ltd., of Avonmouth imported the Canadian Witte Portable Power Drag Saw, best described as an opencranked petrol-engined cross-cut, with blades at six, eight and nine feet long. These saws mounted on two wheels could be dogged on to a large butt, chuffing away for hours, slowly but surely cutting up huge trunks and becoming very popular in sawmills at that time. Scarsbrook's had one. At the outbreak of the war, when imports ceased, Canavon made their own, almost an identical saw called The Avon, now fitted with pneumatic tyres and an attachment for felling. They had one of these, too.

Until recently I had not heard of Scarsbrooks, but I had heard the legend of the giant Cedar of Lebanon at Blenheim, as had others, but none seemed to know who had felled and hauled it until Bernard Berrows, who had seen the huge tree, englightened me. This cedar was growing in the Park gardens and at that time was reputed to be the largest Cedar of Lebanon in Great Britain. It died after the hard winter of 1947. The following summer, Scarsbrooks undertook the massive task of felling and removing it. Remember chainsaws and hydraulic forks were not around; it was the day of the axe, cross-cut and skid load. Jack Scarsbrook prepared to fell the tree with the Avon. First, he welded two six-foot blades end to end giving a twelve-foot cut. Next, they axed round the spurs and set in the fall. The Avon then

*God's Giant parked in Woodstock overnight*

Courtesy of M.L. Marsh

64

commenced its nine-foot diameter cut and its most arduous task. Both the FWD and Crossley took equal strain to prevent pinching or 'sit back' as some fallers call it. The Avon was cutting just seven hours before the 'King of Cedars' came down and broke up with one almighty roar. An outside Broadcast Unit from the BBC was in attendance to record the fall, but were unable to keep the seven hours vigil. Photographs show the giant tree as the lad started with his seven-pound axe and a fine craftsman he was, too, I'm told. The treetop rendered over forty tons of cordwood and there was a thousand cubic feet of merchantable timber in the upper limbs alone. At the crown, the butt was fourteen feet across and cut at eighteen feet long. The girthing was twenty-eight feet six inches (straight measure). As for the Avon, the cut was clean and true. The firm featured its achievement in its sales literature. The gigantic butt was loaded and brought up into Woodstock and parked overnight in the town centre for public viewing. Back at the yard, it was unloaded and the plan was to rip it down-grain one day with the Avon twelve footer, but somehow they never did and after twenty four years, when the yard was sold in 1972, it remained nearly as sound as the day it was felled, thanks to a sheltered location. However, finally the Blenheim giant was chain-sawed up for firewood.

I looked again hard and long at the heavily loaded Tasker, the much enlarged photograph, framed in the original cedar of course, and I remembered Bernard Berrow's comments, "I saw that tree — Load and haul that and you can call yourself a timber-carter". He should know having hauled as many big trees as any of us. A young lady once saw timber haulage as moving "God's Giants", this tree was one of them.

Scarsbrook's was truly a family firm in every sense of the word. Fred, his wife, Lily, all the sons and even the daughters played their part, and this book would not be complete without them.

*Nigel's F.W.D. with the giant cedar*

*A big tree for a light trailer*

*Puny man with God's Giant*

*The Avon starts its seven hour cut*

*Now for some axe muscle (note 12 ft. saw blade)*

# Shoulders to the wheel

The estate sawmill at Woburn, Beds has closed, yet another sad sign of our times. Ken Parker, the head forester, sent me to find Ernest Peacock, who is ninety-six years old and started on the estate when he was sixteen. He remembered the yard opening and must have brought some of the first timber into it. He kept working until he was seventy-two and he recollected when over sixty men worked throughout the woods at one time.

An old steam lorry collected faggots for use in the Abbey. They were stacked in large ricks and four or five men would work daily all the year round chopping the faggots and bundling them up. His friend, Mr. Norman, an ex-sawyer and a mere seventy years old, spoke of Ernest's gift in handling his horses. It was as if they almost listened to his quiet command. Apparently, he had two favourites Punch and Sure. One young two-year-old was extra strong and Ernest had to run to keep up with the horse even when the horse was pulling a load, but was no good working with the others in a team. Instead of anticipating the job and working with them, he would pull madly in his own way and upset the rest, like some people we all know.

I asked Ernest, "Considering the mud, working in all weathers, the risk to life and limb, would you do the same if you had your time over again?" He replied, "Well, we had some happy times and we were contented. We had a good club down at The Magpie. Old Anstey from Cranfield would bring four or five chara's for outings with the old wicker barrel in the back", he said smiling.

In the course of meeting timber men, I've seen many pictures of timber haulage scenes in their homes. One such, faded with age, depicts a team of horses struggling to get a load over the brow of a hill. The old carter is at one of the huge rear wheels spread-eagled across the centre hub grasping the spokes as he assisted their turning. "Shoulders to the wheel", I quipped, Ernest gave me a hard look of rebuke, saying, "That pound or two on the wheel could make all the difference between getting up a hill or not. I've had to do that many times".

Cyril Read could account for the later days. The first tractor was a T.V.O. standard Fordson, next a Major, followed by a Ford Northrop Conversion. Then came a most unusual timber tractor, a giant Dutra of Hungarian manufacture. The double drum winch was replaced by a Boughton ten ton model. Cyril took her over when she was new, and drove her almost up to the time when the yard was closed. The Dutra would pull five hundred cubic feet with ease and winching out loads became a thing of the past. One could hook up with confidence in very wet conditions. In fact, her power (85 HP) was such that he found that if he was not very careful she would churn away turning the wheels within the stationary tyres. Apart from a few minor points, he had nothing but praise for the Dutra.

I looked again over the locked gates, closed as is a whole chapter in the Bedfordshire timber industry, but one thing is sure I will never again talk glibly about shoulders to the wheel without remembering Ernest Peacock. He knew the real meaning of the phrase.

*Ernest Peacock — Woburn June 1951*

Reproduced by kind permission
of The Forestry Commission

*T.V.O. Fordson similar to Woburn saw mills outfit*

*Astells hauling elm in Wrest Park Silsoe, Beds.*
Reproduced by kind permission of Luton Museum and Art Gallery

68

# A pair of Trumpet Horns

At the close of my interview with Tim Powell, son of the founder of Universal Power Drives, he was packing away photographs not relevant to the forestry scene when a small and now crumpled snapshot fell out. It was of a Hannibal tractor with a rare load. Someone had sent it to the Company to confirm their product's potential in action. Nothing was written on the back to indicate the source. The sign writing on the cab was no longer clear, but it was definitely Kent and the name looked like Spain under magnification. The hunt for a Unipower operator in Kent of that name was now on.

Alfred Spain of Ashford was well known in Kent and Sussex timber and heavy haulage circles. In fact, whenever recovery or abnormal road transport was required in those parts, he often got the job. This was back in the late twenties. His lad, young David, often went with dad and was brought up to the rigours of moving big trees with a variety of steam tractors. It therefore followed that when he was fifteen years old, part-time became full time. He featured on many of the early photographs as did the dog, who went everywhere with Alfred and loved to ride on the steamers.

David took over the business at nearby Kennington in 1947, having married in 1944. His wife, May, discovered she had not only gained a husband but an active part in a small, but heavy and tough business. She was to become first reserve when labour was short, from laying out chains and other mates' jobs to hand-burning tree tops in the woods to make clearance for loading, a job not to be confused with the average garden bonfire or pushing of brushwood with a tractor fork. This was nothing more than the hot slog of stumbling over cordwood and humping branches, often in one's own smoke, a killing job. Being tea-girl to the fallers and drivers was just another chore. Indeed, May Spain had her share of timbering.

There are many photographs of their Latil ELL180 with which David hauled all over the South East. One day, came the challenge. He was asked if he could take about 300 cubic feet of special timber for boat building from Maidstone to Barrow-in-Furness. To this he agreed, using the Latil. He loaded one morning, rested, then met the police who were to escort him through a difficult area and then came the road to London and the North to say nothing of the long night ahead. Suffice to say, the trip went all right as did many more when required. That old Latil often chugged and screamed the northern trip at 20 mph flat out, proudly proclaiming from the sign over the cab, "Timber Transport from Forest to Mill". There must have been many tales of the 'Barrow Marathon', but I was not privileged to meet David Spain. Those who have driven a pre-war Latil on say a thirty-mile basis will know they were harsh, hard vehicles to hold on the road. The strain on the ears, arms, shoulders and ribs could become intolerable, whilst braking was mostly dependent on nifty gear changes through the box from top to bottom. There were spur wheels to be greased each sixty miles and various other adjustments, all to be considered against the background of a run like this.

Later, David ran an ex-USA 6 × 6 GMC Artic., plus an early Unipower. The day came when a brand new gleaming Hannibal was delivered and was linked to a Tasker six-wheeled carriage. It lacked just one thing and so David fitted a beautiful pair of trumpet horns on the front wings. By now a lot of dad was coming out in David. He was specialising in pulling and hauling awkward trees and overwide loads that

*Latils were never intended for loads like this*

70

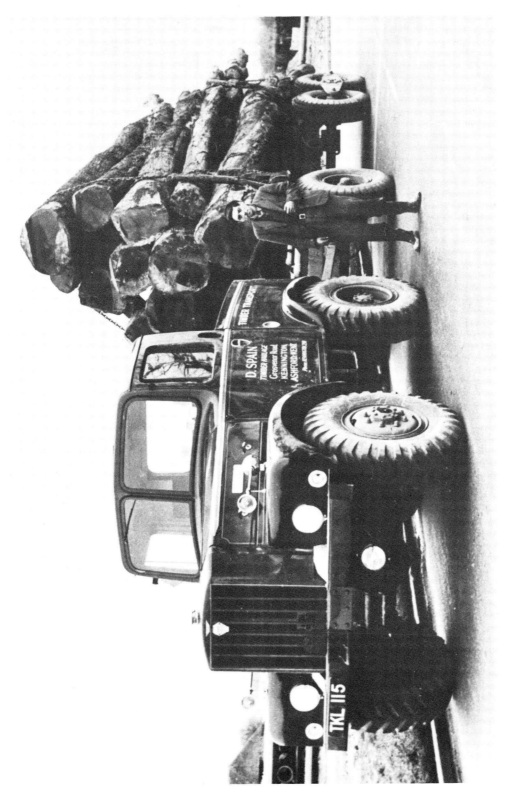

*The Hanibal Trumpet horns and all*

71

regularly took him along the narrow lanes of his native Kent. He made sure they would hear him coming with the blast from those twin trumpets to the background purr of a Gardner 5LW in full song. Now there is music for you.

For several years, David enjoyed collecting a giant Christmas tree from the point of its growth, transporting and helping to erect it with the Unipower in the town centre for the special Ashford Children's Day. His hobby, when time permitted was grass-track racing. Much of the David Spain story will never be told as sadly he contracted an illness from which he did not recover, but at least we have these marvellous photographs. How fortunate for us 'that chap from Kent' sent that little snapshot to Unipowers and that it fell out in my presence that day.

Imagine a directory of timber hauliers Par Excellence. Right there at the top of the S's surely would be the names of Alfred and David Spain.

*The G.M.C. Artic and Unipower*

*Alfred and David Spain*

*From Maidstone to Barrow-in-Furness — hundreds of screaming miles!*

*Alfred's sentinel*

*An unexpected confrontation*
*in Chilham Woods*

*From Forest to Mill*

*"Talk about axle weight"*

73

# Roots

When Mr. W. G. Binder (Snr) of Cryers Hill, High Wycombe, was made redundant from his building job, he built his own house on the plot of land given to him as a wedding present. The idea, originally, was to sell it and build another and another and so on, but it didn't work out that way. However, a professional businessman asked him to build a house like it and steadily through recommendation so did many others, so the end result was the same. There was just one problem; all these properties were to be situated in their own heavily wooded, beech-laden Chiltern areas. This meant that many trees had not only to be felled, but had to be grubbed out by the roots, and so it was that a small team of land clearance men-cum-builders was formed. The timber was brought back to the yard where it was converted to chair legs and logs, making a winter time job since they did not build during the frosty months before the war, all over fifty years ago. Today, his son, Ted Binder, heads a specialist land-clearance company at the same address. Picks, shovels, axes, and a monkey-winch have given way to two giant Volvo loading forks, a twenty-two-ton Caterpillar 977, low loaders, dump trucks, root-grinders and winches galore.

If timber haulage is tough, and it is, getting them out by the roots is tougher. Have you ever tried loading big trees with roots still attached? Binders frequently did. This photograph is a shot of their Unipower Hannibal nosing out such a load, with the root, even cleaned, still eleven feet wide. It gives a little idea of their everyday jobs. They first dug with a Chaseside Shovel, whilst an FWD and an early petrol Unipower all came before the Foden STG5, new in 1950, and incidentally still doing a day's work when required for the Bucks Traction Engine Rallies, ferrying coal.

A unique winch-tractor which is in the fleet today is a Leyland 4 × 4 with twenty ton winch, powered by a 375 engine. It is a prototype for the army and after field trials, it joined the forces of the stubborn-root-brigade at Cryers Hill. In February, 1982, she left the yard for Worksop, Notts., to pull trees out and remove them from an island in the middle of a lake. Ted Binder has nothing but praise for this little winch soon to be replaced by a Bedford 4 × 4. I said little winch, but so it is compared with the big one. Out in the yard stands EBH 724F AEC 6 × 6 (Militant type) whose 11.3 engine powers a Boughton fifty-ton hydraulic-operated winch, crane and anchor and which is just about the biggest purpose built timber-winch ever made in the U.K. At today's costs it would be £70,000 plus, indeed the daddy of them all if ever there was one. It is a sort of when-all-else-fails machine — a D8 debogger. Very little resists this vehicle when those giant anchors take the strain.

For years now, Ted Binder has lived by looking at huge trees and deciding how big and heavy the root will be, how tight, for they vary according to the soil, and how his tackle will take to loading and transporting the root to dump it. It is a testing job for nerve, limb, and pocket alike. True, root-grinding has now taken much of the sting out of the job, but looking back he says, "Root grubbers should expect a free pass to heaven since they've already suffered enough down here". Well, he should know, he's done as much rooting as anyone, the writer would wager.

74

*New from Fodens 1950*

*Another Binder load*

*The 4 × 4 prototype Leyland*

*The Militant Persuader*

75

# Latil — the French connection

"Move off when I say and keep going no matter who gets in the way" ordered a policeman, oddly enough, seated up on a Latil with revolver in hand. The place was the London Docks, the time the General Strike, the driver Colin Riekie's father. It was Colin's first recollection of a Latil. His father had joined the London-based company in 1924. The tractors then were imported direct from France and of the type used in World War 1, 4 × 4 monsters with huge cast wheels, with capstan winches and a petrol consumption of two to three mpg. Although quite capable of pulling twenty tons with only a transmission brake and water tanks and tap to keep it cool, the brakes left much to be desired as father found when one ran away with him in Forest Hill. It was at this time that Colin's father set off for Liverpool with a huge trailer of flour from the docks.

Colin's father served as engineer, salesman and demonstrator and was well known throughout the timber trade. It is interesting to note that when Sir Nigel Gresley approached Latil with his idea of a road-rail shunting tractor, it was Colin's father who designed the rail-wheel assemblies and made the prototype. Colin enthused as he recalled the thrill of an eleven year old lad being allowed to ride in the cab as father drove the first one up the Great West Road to the famous Firestone Tyre Factory and how they were filmed as the unusual machine virtually ascended the steps over to the rail siding and on to the line.

Demonstrating Latils throughout the British Isles, Mr. Riekie once won a medal in Ireland for ploughing, although he had never ploughed before. The site was so wet that the Latil tractor with its 4 × 4 qualities was the only one able to perform at all.

The driver who had perfected the art of killing a rabbit with a catapult and a minute ball-bearing from the seat of his open-fronted, canvas-topped old Latil took over a new, normal cab-model, forgot himself, took aim and tried to get his bunny through the screen, which suffered somewhat from his efforts.

Colin's father became friendly with Colonel Scammel. It seems Latils were giving the War Office a demonstration at the army proving grounds and the Latil on one occasion had to debog a heavy Scammel that was well and truly stuck. Mr. Riekie became involved in the development of the Ford-engined mechanical horse and later Colin went to join him at Jensons of West Bromwich, where they were both responsible for many car and commercial projects for twelve years, but even so, many will remember Mr. Riekie best as the Latil service engineer who travelled to most of their machines in his impressive white Marmod straight-eight car.

During the early 1930s, there is no doubt that the Latil winch-tractor had no real rivals either on or off the road. Nothing else had four-wheel drive and steering plus a differential lock and low ground pressure. It was the answer to many a timber man's dream and the efforts of Mr. Riekie played no small part in making that dream come true.

Colin had looked forward to another session with me when he was to have completed his father's story, but sadly he passed away before this was possible.

# Fodens for ever

S. Darke and Sons of Worcester were well known throughout the Midlands so I was more than a little surprised that they could not be located. Perseverance finally paid off, when I was directed to one, Ron Morgan. Len Darke, one of the two sons, married Ron's sister and Ron had spent most of his life in timber with the Darkes. The other son, Tom, was killed in a timber-haulage accident. — Another grim story repeated so often while this book was being researched. Len Darke, also, is now dead. Ron offered to come up to Eaton Bray bringing his close friend and former tractor mate, Ben Hinton. The highlight of the visit was Ron producing a projector, screen and three hours of slides based on various vehicles of the Darke fleet in action. I warm still to that marvellous afternoon of armchair timber hauling. Ron left me with much of his story still untold and therefore a further meeting was agreed. Sadly that was not to be. Shortly afterwards, he collapsed and died and this book is the poorer for that. These photographs, some from slides loaned by his wife and some by Ben, tell yet another story of timber men.

Mr. Darke senior had a tipper, not the sort that has hydraulic-ram troubles, but a horse-drawn one. He carted sand and ballast round Worcester. Expanding, he went into timber haulage with several teams of horses. His yard was on one side of Worcester, the stable and field on the other. Each night and morning, a horse-keeper would mount one of the horses and drive fifteen to twenty horses loose and free of rein and halter right through the city centre. We do not know the date of this, but anyone who has attempted to drive through Worcester lately will know it was not in recent years.

Of steam, Ron remembered a selection of several engines, some of which are in preservation today, including an ex-showman's engine named Starlight, one of the 3D Type Fodens, and a little 5 HP Burrell called, 'I can hop it'. Ron drove first the Foden pictured here and had many stories including the one about the farm they were working on where the steam coal was dumped beside the hen house, which it seems a mate would frequent to extract eggs. He slipped up one day by visiting the nests after loading the coal. In an angry confrontation, the farmer showed him the trail of coal dust across the hen run and in the nest box and bellowed, "Now don't try to tell me you are not having the eggs". Getting out on the road one day, they lost the pin, or dog as they called it, that locks through from the winch to the drive wheel. An old lady saw the driver searching the road and enquired what was lost. "A dog, ma'am" came the reply. "I've seen no dog. What sort is it?" she asked. "A big black, greasy one" came the final word from the driver. The old lady shook her head "I'm sorry", she said, "I've seen no dog like that round here."

Two TG5 chain-drive diesel Fodens were the pride and joy of Tom Darke and the two Latils came on the scene also around this time, one with a traditional cab the other with a canvas top. Darke's carpenter built a cab for this machine after the following incident. Normally, Ron drove one Latil and Ken Darke the other. One day when the one with the canvas top was only a month old, they were working thirty miles away with Ron as mate to Len on that occasion. The Latil was winching out a big oak on the side of a hill. In spite of all their care, the big tree slewed around and started to roll towards the tractor. Len was in the throes of moving out when the mighty oak hit the Latil sideways on, turning it over completely. Ron remembers well seeing how the inverted side opening of the Latil body now looked like the entrance to a dog kennel. How relieved he was to see Len crawl out on all fours in true doggy fashion. Ron ran over to nearby woods where their Foden was working. They turned the Latil upright, threw the broken hood, windscreen and bonnet on the back of the Latil, and loaded the troublesome oak. They waited for dusk, for appearance's sake, and then drove home and delivered the would-be-killer tree. "We were shaken", said Ron, "but we seldom went home without a load".

For a short period, Ron worked for Latil UK in London, having the use of a French-made 15 cwt service-van. He remembered giving several forestry demonstrations and recalled a few agricultural shows where it was the practice of the company to dig a circular trench around their stand, drive a tractor's front and nearside wheels into it, set the machine in bottom gear and allow the vehicle to rotate slowly at a fast tick over, unattended. This was an impressive sight.

Darke's built most of their own trailers. As Ron said, "You want a good back end. That's where the weight goes". One such super unit was called Big Ben as it was the tandem unit of an ex-Thorneycroft Big Ben forty-ton unit. The Big Ben tractor was next to the top of the heavy range beside the Antar. That trailer carried thousands of cubic feet and is still around today having served with many tractor-units.

As retirement neared, Ron concentrated on winching and loading on the Matadors, a task he appeared to accept grudgingly, but that is hardly surprising. Foden D Types were his great love. Ron Morgan was a true man of steam. At Darke's there were two Geoffs, so when Geoff Hinton went there in 1946, he took on his father's name, Ben, to prevent confusion. He was another old timber man, and apart from the time when he went and helped in the Marines (National Service) he remained with Darkes. Ron Morgan had shown him the ropes (and chains) with the various petrol and diesel Unipowers. But the days of tractor and trailer were numbered and Ben's future lay with various vehicles including a Foden eight-legger and Leyland Octopus bolster-wagon.

One odd ball was an ex-WD Thorneycroft 6 × 4 tractor unit, quite likely one of the few special Nubians made, powered by Thorneycroft's own four-cylinder diesel, a good puller but somewhat smoky, with the manifold exhaust-pipe right on the driver's left leg, which kept it hot in winter and scorching at all other times. Now the army had already fitted good springs on the tandem back end, but they were not good enough for the loads Darke's envisaged, so the springs were set up well, so much so that the prop-shaft to the rear double-drive fouled the necessary chassis cross-member when the unit was without load. Therefore, an added duty for the driver was to fit the prop-shaft after loading and remove it before unloading at the other end, a job Ben could do with speed after practice, not counting wet days I guess.

Fodens with Gardner 180 engines, Leyland 680 fastest in the fleet, and a two-stroke — Ben had them all at different times, but it was the two-stroker that got him going. Or was it the other way round? Whichever way it was Ben enthused about this amazing machine. From the start she was matched to the Big Ben trailer. Darke's knew Big Ben would carry all the Foden could pull. For her first job she was taken to a bad site which required the ascending of a steep hill to get off the job. Having been loaded with a real Darke-type load, Ben was reminded of his instructions which were, 'Keep that foot down and keep her revving well', and he did just that. The Foden virtually sailed up out of that job or should I say roared, as she took the incline with her super load, but the important point is that the two-stroker came back for

*Walnuts to Worcester*

more and more and more. Ben and his Mark 7 turbo-charged Foden had become firm friends. Its matching twelve-speed box and all made eight hundred cubic feet a comfortable load for both man and motor. If Ben Hinton were to appear on Desert Island Discs, Beethoven's Fifth Symphony would never be his choice. Music to his ears I am sure would be a selection of sounds played on a twelve-speed box fitted to a Foden two-stroke as she ascended a mountain pass. "But, surely the Foden two-strokes were nothing but trouble", I said. Ben shook his head, "I'll speak as I find. In thousands of miles she only required two cylinder-head gaskets". Looking again at the pictures of the Foden fleet, his final remark was, "They started with Foden and they finished with Foden". Today, Ben is still in timber, driving an X registration MERC, no propshafts to refit these days. The Darke story is one of great interest and in my book centres on RON and BEN, the Foden men.

*Hilda — a Foden D type*
*with its massive load*

*Two rare Latil loads*

*A war time scene (note headlamp mask)*
Reproduced by kind permission of Mr. Williams, Kingsland Sawmills

80

*A nicely loaded Leyland*

*The Leyland eightlegger octopus*

*Ben Hinton with 800 cube
on the Foden two stroke*

*Foden fleet line up*

# We were only old boys

Few people today remember round timber haulage by horses. Far fewer still remember going with them. Frank Perridge can. Putting another log on the sitting room fire in his home at Shefford in Bedfordshire, Frank, on his eightieth birthday, put back the clock as his lively mind relived scene after scene from his fascinating life in timber. He went to school until he was thirteen and at an early age learned his craft, from emptying sawdust pits to saw-doctoring, in the little mill his father founded at the rear of his present home. Around his sixteenth birthday, Frank started out on the road with a team of horses. "We were only old boys", said Frank referring to the lads he used to meet with another horse-team which came from Bedford. Lads were in charge of Shire-type horses, hefty animals bred to pull a ton and a quarter each. I say Shire-type since Frank felt Shires themselves were good pullers in rough woods, but less able to stand the long road journeys. They were a sort of Latil of the horse world.

Frank walked many miles, since the average day would take them thirty miles or more. He vividly recalls taking a load to the Great Northern Saw Mills at Huntingdon, twenty three miles away on a bitterly cold winter's day. He left at 4 a.m. returning tired at 8.30 p.m. It was little wonder that many a horse and man lost their lives when timber carting. Those who have tried it, know the risks of chopping a partly loaded tree on a waggon to get the bolster-pin in, even with a twenty-ton winch holding the load to inspire confidence. How much more risky it is when one has to trust a team of horses not to relax their hold. Implicit trust was indeed the order of the day.

Frank recalled one night when he had a longish load. The whip of the tree-tails blew out the old red hurricane lamp which he brought up to the rear bolster. Twelve feet was the agreed legal length beyond the end of the pole after dark. When the representative of the law appeared and inferred that the limit was somewhat stretched, Frank attempted to bluff him with a two-foot rule as he proceeded to measure, allowing the rule to slip back each move in the darkness. As the constable became aware of this, he sent him on his way with a few stern words for his cheek.

Even today, in Silverstone, they talk of Frank's uncle, a timber carter who worked for a firm that owned forty horses and hauled from as far off as Wales. Returning from there one Saturday night, he stopped at a pub in Banbury at nine o'clock to rest the team. After watering and nosebagging them, he entered the Inn for his own refreshment. On returning, he recalled climbing on to his chaff-sack seat and setting off. At this point, he must have fallen into a very deep sleep for he remembered no more until he was awakened at 4.30 a.m. on Sunday morning, when the horses stopped back home in the yard seventeen and a half miles away. The team had made its way, unguided or driven by anyone for the whole journey, which included going through the town of Brackley. That is horse-sense.

One grim job entailed extracting trees from a bog. Direct line pulling just ploughed the butts in. Cunningly, Frank rolled them out without a hitch. With the advent of steam, a new fangled Foden from another firm arrived for trees they had purchased there. One good pull and into the bog the new steamer went and stayed for a few days resisting all efforts of recovery. The Company sent in their horse team to complete the job and one day arranged with Frank to fire up the Foden so the wheels would turn. Then with an elaborate snatch-block set-up, they mustered their own team and Frank's, thirteen horses in all. They pulled with one great continuous heave and the heavy steamer was freed from the captive bog.

If a picture ever tells a story it is the one on Frank's wall. The giant tree is a huge burr-brown oak, gale-blown in Silsoe Park. Some indication of its size is realized in that Frank's father paid £95 for it back in 1932. Far too large for any saw of his, he offered it to many timber merchants, all of whom wanted it until they saw its size. Then all lost interest for the same reason. None had a saw big enough to tackle the brute. Finally, it was sold for export to Canada. The Railway agreed to take it to London Docks if it was delivered to Southill Station. Frank and his father knew of only one haulier who might tackle this difficult task. It was Tommy Nowlton of Elstow because he had what he called "a big engine". They got out the old bullnose Morris and fetched Tommy over. He sized up the problem and risks of such a great load, fixed a price, and with his skilled driver, Olly, and the big engine, safely transported the tree.

At this point, Father Perridge and Tommy's troubles should have been over, and were, until a Railway official saw the massive 'stick' and decided however it was laid, it was far too wide for their big bolster trucks. However, since the Railway were now committed, they offered to pay Tommy £20 to take it to the docks for them. Now it's one thing to do a few miles down country lanes, but quite another to go forty odd miles into London with a tree measuring around 600 cubic feet at something like 28 cubic feet to the ton. It was grossly over-wide for Tommy's timber drug, and a heavy and indivisible load if ever there was one. Frank rose early and fired the engine for a 4 a.m. start. His father, Tommy, and Olly set off with the daunting load and were safely back after dinner next day. It must have been a great relief to all three, and to the big engine, as the four-inch thick hemp rope-slings lifted the Silsoe giant and swung it another step toward the larger saws of Canada.

Driver Olly's skills were again tested, when he commenced descending a hill with two timber drugs in tow, one being hooked to the pole of the other with about 200 cubic feet on each. Frank as mate, diving over the pole from wheel to wheel, was not winding on the brakes quickly enough and as the outfit gathered speed, the smoke-box door came open and chains, skids and hooks littered the road. Somehow Olly kept the engine straight and the disaster of a double jack-knife was avoided. Breathlessly, Frank collected the missing tackle and they went on their way.

As steam yielded to petrol, tiny tractors, when compared with their contemporaries, originating from France, started to appear bearing the name Latil. The first one Frank saw had a canvas hood and knock-over wheel-cleats or spuds. A potential customer was having a demonstration and had cannily asked the Latil men to extract three elm trees from the middle of a very wet wood whilst he tackled a quick easy load near the road with his steamer. Imagine his amazement when the Latil staff winched their loaded drug on to the road and came back and politely offered to finish loading the Foden steamer. Small wonder that a Latil sale was gained that day and a repeat order for two more later.

The Perridge name was on a Fordson tractor and later an ex-WD Crossley fitted with winch and anchors. Although he liked her, Frank's comments were "Fast but thirsty".

Frank took me to Silverstone to meet his old friend, Jim Linnell, who heads the family-owned sawmill. He was busy in the Sharp Shop, the saw doctor's, at eighty-eight years. He only sharpens three or four a day now. Jim has done the lot in his time. He excelled in buying standing timber. Trees can grow in a wood all appearing to be of a similar size and nature, yet when they are felled they can vary much in quality owing to ground conditions. Jim has the gift of digging a couple of spits by a spade nearby and knowing in a moment how that tree will appear when felled. 'Laggy' or shake running up the grain often renders a fine tree almost useless. He has saved pounds in his time. "Watch out for 'Ickle' holes", he warned, the local name for woodpeckers. "They can lose you money in a moment."

It was never intended as a personalized number plate, but as his car registration letters were ETM, other members of the English Timber Merchant Association often ribbed Frank about the coincidence. In his garden lies an old SAMPSOM. Before the days of winches it was the only manual way to turn or pull a leaning tree. It was a simple implement with a five-foot handle-shaft mounted into an iron socket with three hooks on short chains working on the same principle as the modern load binder, Twitch, or Wrister as they call it down Gloucester way. As they say, nothing is new under the sun.

One could be forgiven for expecting Frank Perridge to be doubled up with arthritis. Not a bit of it. Today, he still uses a chainsaw to cut his own logs. He is never happier than when he goes back to Silverstone, the Northants village of numerous sawmills and the name of Frank's present house and his father's old home. It is the place where he loves to meet old friends, see the newest techniques, and the electronic console of the latest bandmill. He is truly amazed by the tremendous changes over all the years since he was 'only an old boy'.

*Tommy Nowlton's Big Engine*

*Frank Perridge and Jim Linnell, Silverstone 1982*

84

# The toughest man in timber

"Our governor is the toughest man in timber" are words I still remember, after thirty years, and were spoken by two men in a West of England transport cafe, whose red, Devon mud-stained overalls made me realise that they were hauliers as I was. The name on their unit coupled to a huge load outside was that of Henry Giles of Bath.

The Giles story took me to Marksbury near Bath to meet grandson Roger, Tom Shellard and Edgar Jones, affectionatly known as Twink, on a late summer's evening in 1983.

Henry Giles got married about ninety years ago. A local sawmill put up the money for a wagon and team of approximately fifteen horses. Henry's income was a mere pittance and paying back the money to the mill was no easy matter. Although both man and beasts often worked until fit to drop, Henry went bankrupt three times before discharging his debt. His young bride wondered what took him away such long hours until one day she joined him for a day in his life. It was said afterwards that she never again went with him or ever again complained. Guts, the sweat of his brow, and realistic pricing brought Henry success and he was able to buy a T.V.O. Fordson with front-mounted auto-mower winch, followed in due course by a Foden D Type Steam Tractor. At that time, he was hauling into a yard at Midsomer Norton where he saw a future in an eighteen year-old lad, who was working there and who regularly refused to go and work for him. One day, it appears that Henry took the lad to a pub for a drink and somehow young Twink found he had a new boss and belonged to a company with whom he stayed for over forty years.

Henry's eldest son Reginald worked for his father for a while, but later went on his own. It seems there was a friendly sharing of both employees and tackle. Reginald's son Roger did his stint of log cart, however.

It is no secret that Henry Giles took big risks in business, and risked his tackle and his life. He subjected his body to excessive abuse and stress over the years from a smashed thumb, dislocated shoulder, back injuries, and broken ribs and plates in his legs, but by far the worst was when a rope broke and a flying C hook smashed his face and jaw, disfiguring him for life. He boasted hospitals had a parts-manual on his replacements and that little of the original body was left. Henry was once on top of a thirty-foot high huge mound of trees in a timber yard. A complete load of timber was being rolled up the heap by two tractors around the other side. as the drivers took their signals from him, the tree he was standing on moved, causing him to slip down a few feet into the heap. Promptly the drivers stopped, climbed up, and freed him from his perilous trap. Malmesbury Hospital had the honour of fixing him on that occasion.

After the Ford V8-engined auto-tractor, Twink took over the first Leyland Beaver Auto-Winch Tractor made in August, 1946, registered number GL9816. Its 600 engine covered some two hundred thousand miles. Later, a second Beaver was purchased, as was a Foden, ERF, Latil and Unipowers in both Henry's and Reginald's fleet jointly. Twink spoke highly of the Beavers as he did of two Ministry of Supply FWD's on loan through the wartime lease-lend scheme. The FWD's are not to be confused with the petrol Sucoe model we all know, but were two of the eighty-five sent direct from the States with twin rear-wheels powered by a Cummins AA600 engine. Their engines had 100 hp capable of 50 mph and short steel ballast-type bodies, which would just carry their TD 9 crawler. In permanent all-wheel drive and diff. lock one of these vehicles once dragged a 240 cubic feet Scotch Pine along the road without the slightest tyre scrub. As for the standard Garwood winch, it once pulled the TD9 out of a bog when only the air filter was showing.

Twink and Tom recalled the one-in-four hill down at Brendon in the Doone Valley. Henry always sent two sets of tackle to double-up tractors for such gradients. On one occasion, Twink was caught out alone. In reply to his call, Henry said, "Rope her up as best you can", and this he did, roping and zig-zagging with 500 cubic feet, a test of nerve and skill if ever there was one. One crawler driver they remembered was well over seventy years old at the time, the sort of chap who would stand in a stream of water up to his thighs, cranking a tractor like a twenty-one-year-old.

One of Henry's worst jobs was on Exmoor, on the Glenthorn Estate. The three-mile-long road had many hairpin bends and dropped eleven hundred feet in one and threequarter miles. The severity of the bends broke the lockstops on a normal carriage even when shortened right up, so Henry designed and had made a carriage with a turntable at each end operating via a system of linking chains to each turntable. In this way they got out hundreds of cubic feet at not more than one hundred and fifty cubic feet per load. It took months in all weathers. Tom Shelland and his mate lived down there in a converted Bristol single decker. Tom's memories of Glenthorn are legion. They were changing a wheel on the carriage one day when it rolled only two feet to a sheer drop. Down the combe it sped, gathering speed. It ran half way up the opposite bank and lodged in a bush. Just as they set out to get it, the wheel was dislodged and plunged to the bottom. It took hours to retrieve.

A picture of a loaded carriage in disarray was taken after it had rolled over down a bank and landed in the top of a tree growing forty feet below. Had not the tree supported this precarious load it would have dropped a further sixty feet down on to a house. Then there was the day that the 'Charmer' (Allis Model U) went out of control. The brake lever sheered off in Tom's hand with the gear-lever between winch and travel position, the tractor picking up speed and heading for a two hundred feet drop down to the beach. He jumped clear as the tractor hit a stump just yards from the edge. Tom had his camera when called to a twenty-two ton R.B. Dragline in the drink. Bristol Aqua Club fixed a giant hawser to it and three Giles tractors did the rest.

One of the Leyland Beavers took a load up north when the diff. failed. A recovery truck started to tow it to a garage, but en route it was found that the cobbled road up a hill was partially blocked by one of Pickford's outfits, stuck for want of power. Sizing up the situation, the Giles driver said, "I'll get you up." "But you are already on tow", chorused the Pickford driver and the recovery man together. "Maybe, but my winch is still working. Take me up the hill and shove my back end into the curb and I'll rope you up in no time", said the Giles driver, and he did.

A sticker for the Giles tractors might have read, 'We have worked with the lions of Longleat'. Several large oaks were to be removed from the lions' park whilst the occupants were in residence. The Giles men were briefed with care. An armed guard would attend at all times. "Just seeing a rifle upsets the lions", the guards said. "They may just be curious". On the first day, Twink dozed in his cab after dinner and wakened to find a whole family of six lions basking on his flat trailer in the sun. As the job progressed, it became apparent that the chain saws and tackle were annoying the lions more and more. One day, the guard was called away on his radio. Thrusting his rifle in Roger Giles' hands, he said, "Take over for a minute. Let them see it and you'll be O.K." Roger had to cover both himself and Twink. One nasty old lioness became increasingly aggressive, jumping on a loaded tree with snarls all round. Next, she reared up and, striking the tree, nearly overturned the trailer. By now Roger began to wonder at what point he would be justified in firing a warning shot. This certainly was no cat curiosity. At this moment, the guard rushed back, took over the rifle, loaded it and backed the lions away — yes, loaded the rifle. Well, he couldn't leave Roger armed, he confessed.

'Bath man gets his 149th traffic conviction' ran the local headlines. It was a Giles driver booked for another minor timber haulage offence. On this occasion the driver was caught double-heading a big load up a steep hill with insufficient lighting. Carrying big trees often called for small adjustments to the law.

With the demise of the pole waggon, Twink's last vehicle was an AEC Mandator with flat trailer. He regularly ran up from Frome to Bowater's at Sittingbourne with pulp wood. He may not remember much about the day he joined Henry Giles, but he will not soon forget his leaving the firm forty odd years later. A beautiful gold watch is his pride and joy, presented by Mrs. Amy Parsons, Henry's oldest daughter. Her story is written on another page. Rosemary Hucker, Henry's grand-daughter, ran and managed the Company during the years up to the end in 1980.

Few in timber come tougher than Henry Giles of Bath. Fewer still could have taken the knocks he did.

*Henry Giles*

*Henry Giles once said, "We don't charge for widening gateways".*

*Checking the load*

*The twin turntable trailer Henry had made*

*A Leyland Beaver, Unipower, and Matador in unison retrieved this 22 ton dragline*

*Twink with the 750 cube elm at Beaulieu*

88

# Charlie Evans

Public opinion forced timber merchant Frederick (Patent) Applegate and his new-fangled steam-driven sawmill out of Norton St. Philip, near Bath. Owners of thatched cottages were adamant. Locals nicknamed him 'Patent' because of his advanced ideas. Everyone else for miles around was using pitsaws. His grandson, Charlie Evans, was born and bred in the village. A paper round took the lad to the home of George Grist, a marvellous engineer who owned and ran the local Auto-Mower Engineering Company. George Grist had been awarded a medal in 1929 for designing and making an automatic tractor ground-anchor. His variety of timber winches and tractors are praised on other pages of this book. His was the first British company to be engaged in making equipment for the home timber trade. The work force was imbued with the idea of taking great pride in their tasks. It was perhaps most fitting that in 1968, T. H. White of Devizes, a real solid company that has served agriculture over one hundred and fifty years, should take over the firm, which still today make many winches for modern application. So much could and should be written of George Grist. Suffice it to say, he set a high standard of product quality that was the envy of his competitors. Would that more of his calibre abounded in industry today.

Charlie Evans recalled many incidents as when, during the war, the supply of heavy tractor drive-chains ceased, whereupon, in no time, Morris Commercial rear axles were brought in to make shaft-drive conversions. Charlie's apprenticeship with Mr. Grist gave him a good grounding for the years ahead. During his holidays and whilst on leave from the RAF, where he expanded his engineering knowledge, he would go and work for one of Auto-Mowers' customers, Henry Giles.

On demobilization, Charlie accepted a job as a fitter, playing his part in keeping the many Giles wheels turning. Every Giles man had to think for himself. Henry Giles did not want to know about his mens' problems, but rather how they overcame them. Charlie described how in 1950, Henry put him on the train bound for Perivale, London, with £3,500 in his pocket, which he exchanged for BGL 739, a gleaming new Unipower Hannibal, that he drove back to Bath. The tractor was not so gleaming when he took her to Mevagissey in Cornwall, where the mud came up to the cab steps. An ex-Ministry of Supply Austin was rebuilt and tested well by Charlie when he took a 350 cubic foot elm from Castle Combe to London, earning him a halfpenny per cubic foot on all over 240 cubic feet. With no booster gear-box, the 27 hp petrol engine revved well in bottom gear as he zig-zagged to climb the worst hills. Why Austins were fitting their larger 32 hp engines in the Princess car seemed a mystery to Charlie.

As artics took over from tractor-trailers, Charlie converted the big Tasker to a semi-trailer, replacing the vacuum-brakes with air to match up to the AEC Mandator. He devised portable legs for the front bolsters so that the Tasker could stand loaded, freeing the tractor unit for other work. Later on, after he had commenced his own engineering and welding business, Henry Giles' granddaughter, Rosemary Hucker, then running the company approached him with a most formidable task. It was to convert an ex-WD AEC Militant $6 \times 6$ into a big-time tree-mover. This involved fitting a large Auto-Mower timber winch into the chassis in such a way that it would stay there when one opened up the 11.3 litre engine under the bonnet. Making up and fitting an anchor that would not buckle when the ten-ton great hulk sat back on it was an achievement in itself. As for the jib, he had to design and make one in keeping with this large machine, yet one which would be agile enough to raise and lower it without a major operation. We are talking about a tractor that would go anywhere and that is said to have a 20,000 lb drawbar capacity. Well, Charlie did the conversion and made a magnificent job of it. No one has ever overtaxed the line pull of the winch. Regarding the jib, it first took 120 cubic feet of green beech up a steep rise with no loss of front wheel traction. Next, the Militant romped and rolled across a ploughed field with 160 cubic feet of green wood swaying at the top of the jib and still came back for more. In the shortest radius, that is three feet, 200 cubic feet would not be impossible. In fact, when the 750 cubic foot elm tree was loaded at Beaulieu on the Mandator, the Militant took the heavy end with a lift and roll load, the special leg supporting the front bolster. An excellent one-man-conversion. Much later, when the engine failed, Charlie himself carried out a complete internal overhaul, afterwards taking 'Millie' from Bath up to a job at Worcester. Charlie Evans is a marvellous welder and engineer I am told, but then perhaps he should be. His schooling was with Grist and Giles.

*The converted AEC Militant — Charlie's brain child*

*Bombed in Bath 1940, Charlie helped rebuild this ERF's cab*

*Charlie with the ex Ministry Austin*

*Men, mud and machines in Mevagissey*

*Leyland Beaver Auto Tractor*

*The Mandator and Tasker*

# Reg and the Macks

Charlie Evans remembers Reg. Hawkins, whose time in timber spans something like fifty years, from horse to H.G.V. His snapshot of one of the few ex-USA Mack's 6 × 6 tractors that served in timber is unique. He took over the vehicle when it was new. Auto Mowers had fitted a good jib to match the Garwood winch. Later, when this became troublesome, Mr. Grist fitted one of the twenty or more winches he had made for the big UK-built postwar Latil. To test it, Reg hooked up to a 400 cubic foot beech, reared the great Mack up and applied the winch brake, but to his disappointment, the Mack slowly returned to the ground. "No problem," said George Grist adjusting the winch brake, and again Reg reared the ten-ton American giant, braked and stayed in mid-air as long as he wished. You can imagine the pasting that jib was taking. It was another feather in the Grist cap, as was the unusual Leyland Beaver and ten-ton pole-trailer Reg also drove.

He told me the nine foot width of the Mack was a problem at first. It appeared the police said he would require an escort each time on the road. This insistence mellowed eventually, when he was limited to a range of forty-mile radius which was well within the area his firm required of him.

Reg soon realised two important features of the air-brakes. One was that the slightest touch would be inclined to thrust him and any passenger towards the windscreen at great force. The second was that this sudden braking had a similar effect on any other road-user following at what he thought a reasonable distance. Many will remember, when air-brakes were first used in the UK, some vehicles carried a little plate at the rear warning 'Caution — Air-brakes', or, as some wit once worded it, 'If I stop, can you?'. But I digress. I heard elsewhere of a similar Mack, used for hauling, whose great front bumper would nudge up to another loaded outfit in front as each ascended a steep hill. That old Mack in six-wheel-drive would push the front load up as well as bringing up her own 500 cubic feet. Another Mack episode concerned an FWD. A high stump had buckled the track-rod as they emerged from a gateway with her load. A garage sent out a Mack breakdown vehicle which took the FWD and trailer with 400 cubic feet in suspended tow. This long awkward procession arrived safely back at the sawmills, thanks in part to the two sixty-gallon petrol tanks whose contents quenched the thirst of the 170 bhp engine.

In 1900, the Mack Brothers in Brooklyn commenced making substantial commercial vehicles. In 1984, many acknowledge this and none more than Reg Hawkins, a Mack man if ever there was one.

*Leyland Beaver and 10 ton pole trailer which Reg Hawkins also drove*

*Reg with a Mach 6 × 6*

# Born 1752 — still going strong

Two Glastonbury Churches feature fine woodwork by a local craftsman, Frank James. He was manager at the sawmill founded right back in 1752 by John Duffett Snow. Later, Frank, along with his brother, A. C. S. James, and T. A. Curtis, was able to buy the major share-holding in the company assisted by the proceeds of an invention of his, which was a reciprocating saw, known as the James Patent. Edward N. James, current managing director, a grandson, gave me a full and fascinating history of what must be the oldest and largest company still in timber to have a place in this book.

I had seen John Snow's tackle around the West Country in the 1950's and wondered whether they had survived. My arrival at Glastonbury was a revelation. Mr. Edward James was in Sweden buying timber, but his daughter, Elisabeth, knowing of my mission, took me off to meet Frank Cook and Harold Lee. This, my briefest of interviews, left me fascinated beyond words. One could sense the pride of these men as they described how, years ago, two steam tractors and carriage had somehow ascended nearly to the peak of Glastonbury Tor, five hundred feet high, a great hill that was thickly wooded in those days. I saw photographs to prove it, but no-one seems to know how this major feat was achieved.

Harold Lee carried a folded, faded photograph of a Matador in the Mendips. The outfit had mounted a bank, overturning the load and crushing both driver and tractor. The driver survived after long hospitalisation.

For some forty years, Frank had hauled much of the time. He remembers the famous Ford V8 engined Auto-Tractors being used for pulling by the throwers. They liked them for this job, since the double anchor prevented the usual bucking and rearing. Frank is a great vehicle sentimentalist describing three other ladies in his life, Wendy, Florrie and Lucy (the logger) all Matadors in whose cabs he had spent great chunks of his life. They were tractors from which much had been demanded and which had given so much more in peace-time than ever Whitehall had designed for them in war.

Of the old Leyland Beaver, her life was not a happy one, Frank said. A standing tree had ripped her open but she was far from finished and later with a chassis extension she served as a 6-wheeler flat. He had a big job near Barnstaple and the place almost became his second home. He could tell me not only the exact number of miles between Glastonbury and Barnstaple but how much petrol was needed for the journey and where many of the low gear changes were to be made. Frank's longest load was just one hundred feet from the bumper to his red rag, according to the police. By far his most awkward load was a big oak, shaped like a starting-handle, that was not to be cut owing to the natural bends. It was before the time of jibs and tractor forks. Try as he might, if she went on the front bolster, she would not go on the rear. Almost in despair he tried his last trick. Dispensing with the skids, he overturned the carriage on to the tree and securely chained the two together. Next he winched the tree and carriage back on to its wheels and behold, the awkward tree was not only loaded, but bound on as well.

As a true member of the old brigade, Frank recalled a 'big end' going one day whilst on the road. Draining the oil into an old tin, he dropped the sump, fitted another 'shell' from a box he carried in the cab, filled up and then carried on with, I suspect, no more concern than our modern HCV man shows in changing a bulb.

I heard the story of the driver pulled up by the police for not having a brakeman. His initiative led him to don a coat and cap on a bag of straw secured to the near side seat, a kind of guy-cum-scarecrow, and it worked until his sick mate returned. An FWD and two Mack 6 × 6 also featured in the haulage team. The name of the game was 'Keep them rolling'. Frank Cook and Harold Lee did just that.

In about an hour, I was taking my last glimpse of this massive mill, now covering many acres. The company that had done so much to pioneer timber-framed housing, supplying H.M. Dockyards and shipping, and which was geared to the complete needs of the building and construction industry had completely amazed me. Mr. Edward James put it in a nutshell. "The company has been ready to adapt to new markets and to respond to change instead of fighting it", he said, and there must be a lesson there for all of us.

This book is dedicated to remarkable men and machines. These sons of Somerset have earned their place in it.

*John Snow hauling on Glastonbury Tor (note the base of the memorial on the top of this 500ft hill)*

*The Leyland Beaver when new*

*The way we used to do it. A John Snow felling team*

*How to roll a Matador and survive!*

96

# Galloping Gertie

Thomas Graveson Limited of Carnforth, Lancs, is best known nowadays for the company slogan, "We specialise in 'Talking' rubbish", which appears on the front of each one of Peter Graveson's thirty vehicle waste-disposal fleet. Grandfather Thomas began it all in 1893, literally by accident. A blasting accident in the quarry where he worked left him with his sight impaired and one hand damaged. Undaunted, he somehow acquired some standing coppice-wood near the Lancaster-Kendal canal and, having felled it himself, enlisted the aid of a bargee to get the first load to Kendal for clog-sole making.

By the time of his death in 1916, he had thirty horses hauling timber most of which was brought via the railway to the company's own sawmill at Carnforth. His youngest son, George, on his return in 1919 from army service, took over the running of the company and survived the awful depression of the late nineteen twenties, when trees that had been bought and felled were left to rot and nine draft horses that had cost ninety pounds each went to the knacker for as little as three pounds each.

When business began to improve, George bought his first vehicle, a Latil tractor and trailer, in 1931. Success with it was such that three more outfits followed, one of which George drove back from London to Carnforth in thirteen hours non-stop with no cab and heavy rain all the way. The first artic. was created in 1935 from a second-hand Bedford cattle truck, bought for £75. A bolster replaced the body and a single-axled pole-trailer fitted. By 1944 there were six more Bedfords, two ERF's, a Fordson V8, and a Commer Flat. For doing the 'snigging out' were a Caterpillar 22, two D4's and a David Brown. The company was working on jobs as far apart as Devon and Dumfries. About this period all the Latils were converted to diesel, by fitting Perkins P6 engines which proved very successful. One Bedford worked for eighteen months in Wales on a five-mile round trip necessitating no less than seventy-five gear changes each way. Another Bedford did thirty-eight thousand miles requiring only one new spark-plug. A press cutting describes how a Latil and loaded trailer, negotiating a flooded road besides Ullswater, crashed through the low wall and capsized in the lake. Two of the crew, riding on top of the load, jumped free and just managed to release the driver. Later, the police inspected his log book in which was written: "Left Dalemain 11.00 a.m. Arrived in Ullswater Lake 11.15 a.m."

When, in 1939, a new quarry was opened at Warton, a local heavy haulier found himself in trouble when, attempting to bring the massive crusher up round a steep corner in the village, his outfit came to a standstill. When a Graveson Latil came to the rescue, the haulage crew laughed at the strange vehicle. They soon changed their tune when in four-wheel drive and four-wheel steer it towed the complete outfit up the steep hill.

As the Latils got older, their various adventures took their toll and left everyone of them minus its cab. One old Graveson hand tells of being right up on the anchor, swinging at a big tree, when a slight twist of the wooden cab-frame jammed the clutch pedal. He baled out just before the Latil wound itself over on to its back. The same man tells of an R.B. excavator which stuck in the silt whilst attempting to ford the River Lune at Lancaster at low tide. An enormous recovery truck had been hired for the rescue and Gravesons were asked to provide a Latil to assist. The Latil driver chose a spot to stand on, an old stone slip-way, using his crowbar to provide slots for his anchor. Having waded out to fix their ropes to the 'navvy', both drivers then began to reel in. The recovery truck driver was too hurried, took all the initial strain, and smashed his rope. The old Latil carried on at a tickover, the winch hardly turning. These tactics beat the suction of the silt and slowly reeled the stricken 'navvy' — to the frustrated astonishment of the other driver. On another occasion, the same Latil and crew were called to assist another excavator which had lost its footing and toppled sideways into soft ground. Two D8 Caterpillars had failed to shift it. The Latil driver asked permission to hitch his rope to the jib. Permission having been granted and the rope attached, once again that bottom gear through the winch did the trick, slowly righting the 'navvy' and leaving the onlookers amazed.

In 1951 George Graveson died leaving his son Peter, aged twenty-three, in charge of the business. Like his father he looked ahead for new methods and in 1954 imported from Sweden a lorry-mounted HIAB hydraulic crane that could lift and load trees up to 2 tons — the first to come into the U.K.

In 1956, Peter began a new venture when he successfully pestered Tarmac Limited for the sub-contract to clear the site of the Preston by-pass. One of the machines used was 'Galloping Gertie', the name given to a gigantic Latil TR 120 'Navette' tractor bought second-hand in Scotland, one of only six imported. It was powered by a Gardner 6 LW engine, made under licence in France. Four-wheel drive, four-wheel steer, and dual controls made it very manoeuvrable and enabled the driver to face either way and watch the mighty Garwood winch working. It was mounted on 24-inch wheels and the overhang of the engine prevented the tractor from rearing when winching. Work on the Lancaster by-pass followed on from the Preston job and Gravesons were acquiring a reputation in Civil Engineering circles for quick reliable work.

Hanamog crawlers were bought. The K 90, equivalent to a D 6, but lighter, was equipped with a British-built rooter. The smaller K 60 was acquired after Peter, quite by chance, saw a film showing a hydraulic logging-fork. He drew his own design, submitted it to Hanamog's who made one from scratch and delivered it from Germany in just three weeks. This tool, mounted on a K 60 crawler-shovel, revolutionised the loading and handling of both trees and stumps on to the company's ex-U.S. army 6 × 6 trucks, and enabled brushwood to be cleared up quickly and lifted on to the fire. In 1961, a Caterpillar 944 wheeled tractor was bought and equipped with Graveson-built forks. Far from being redundant, the two remaining Latils were kept busy winching out inaccessible trees and were often called for by main contractors to extricate tractors, lorries or excavators bogged down at undignified angles.

When the A59 was being widened and straightened at Sawley Brow, a temporary diversion had to be built to carry the traffic and the old road was closed. Immediately, Graveson's gang went into action uprooting an avenue of massive old elms. Tractors manoeuvred, power-saws buzzed, and the job was well under way. Meanwhile, the first heavy lorry on the new diversion sank through the tarmac up to its axles and stuck fast. Chaos reigned, but, through the traffic-jam, 'Gertie' was ushered forward and soon winched out the lorry, but, alas, the new road was ruined. There was then a mad rush to clear the old road, now strewn with the debris of the fallen elms, as the traffic waited to return to the original route.

Harthill by-pass, Scotland's first section of motorway, was largely routed through a peat-bog — a peat bog in a wood. For a quarter of a mile through the middle of the wood no crawler could work. A Caterpillar D 8 and scraper got no further than the stream on the edge of the wood, having gone in headlong and failed to surface. Gertie was nearby, being driven, as it happened, by that same 'old hand' mentioned earlier. He fastened his rope to the rear of the scraper and winched the entire outfit out backwards. The trees were Scots pine growing close together. They were all felled high. Gertie was positioned in the wood at a right angle to the line of the road and every stump was winched out into a massive windrow. Only once did Gertie sink into the peat, but she winched herself to safety, using one snatch-block fastened to the raised anchor and a second one fastened to a tree.

Whilst at work on Ecclefechan by-pass, an ex-Army Scamell tractor pulling an even older low-loader, the rear-axle of which had solid tyres, loaded with a 30 R.B. excavator, was trying to drive up a slight incline and out on to the A74. The old Scamell had severe wheel-spin. The driver uncoupled, moved forward and attempted to use his capstan-winch but simply pulled himself backwards toward the trailer. Gertie was summoned. There was nowhere to stand except on the opposite verge of the main road, at a right angle to the Scamell, which was not at all a good practice. However, with the use of a snatch-block and with all the traffic stopped, the old Scamell, trailer, 'navvy' and all came slowly up the rise and turned on to the main road.

The Latils were frequently used to help the 'forks' drivers in difficult places, a steep slope or a bog. The driver would venture forward, to retrieve a root or dig a tree, dangling on the end of the winch rope. At a wave of the hand they would be wound back to safety. Goodness knows what today's Health and Safety Inspectors would have thought of the procedure!

Howard Nunnick of Colne, Lancs has an insatiable appetite for timber tackle. Had he not found and photographed Latil LYE 224 at work, neither you nor I may ever have heard of 'Galloping Gertie'. We are indebted to Sam Ashton of Gravesons for rounding up 'old hands' whose experiences, along with his own, left me truly amazed, in spite of the fund of stories about men, mud, machines and trees I've heard elsewhere.

*Sam Ashton with Gertie*

*Fording at Welshpool 1935*

*A Latil digs in*

*The Reo 6 × 6 (Ex USA)*

*Gertie rescues the 944*

100

# A collision with Kodak

Softly spoken Ted Everett of Quidenham in Norfolk spent over thirty years timber hauling. His claim to have put seven hundred cube behind a Latil was no idle boast. The vehicles he drove had the Meadows petrol-engines replaced with Perkins P6 and then later R6 for even more power, whilst oversize tyres led to faster road speeds. These tractors were coupled usually to Crane, six-wheeled, 15/20 ton drugs. The shots of DUC45 rearing on her anchors were taken on one of the many occasions when Ted had his tractor sitting up and begging. The forward opening doors were a characteristic of the special cabs the company had made especially by a local firm in Norfolk.

In their day, before the Unipowers came, Latils were used for long as well as short journeys. Ted recalls runs as far up as Yorkshire with the scream of the 'diffs', locked in his head for days after. Would there were room here for all his photographs. He had some marvellous shots. The driver of a Kodak van had a brake failure as he rounded a bend at the top of a steep hill and came face to face with a load of timber creeping up the incline. Hitting first the front bolster, then the rear, slowed him down, opening up the side of the van at the same time. Most of Ted's loads were on the long side and mostly overwide with awkward butts on the second layer wide of the pins. A load was parked overnight at the Comfort Cafe. The driver of a lorry they had stopped beside was so scared, he arose at midnight to move his vehicle a few yards away.

The fleet included a few Unipowers. Here a giant elm in Wimpole Park, Royston, has just been loaded. This tree alone cut two hundred coffin sets. A Scammel Artic. gave valiant service. Here she is shown with a hefty, forked horsechestnut; a pole bender if ever there was one.

In thirty years, Ted's worst job was at Luknor Hill near Stokenchurch, Bucks. It was so wet that they had to winch in and winch forward for every move, taking twelve hours to extract and load six trees. Hardest to load was 500 cubic feet of bent oak tops not to be cut owing to their natural bends, loaded before the days of jibs, and calling for all their skill in redirecting the chains and skids. Top cart, an art that always sorted out the real timber loaders from the others, is a craft acquired by few, but big sticks or tops alike, Ted Everett coped and travelled half of England with them.

*A good solid load put on with skids*

*A collision with Kodak*

*Wimpole Park, 762 Cabe Elm (200 coffins)*

*A bonus load of oak*

*Loading a reluctant tree*

*Ted tops up the Scammell*

*A rough "Conker" for the Scammell from Royston to Doncaster*

*Concern at the "Comfort Cafe"*

103

# Chiltern Round-up

## The Brightman Brothers

From Norfolk to Somerset, from Surrey to Worcester, I was asked time after time, 'Do you know the Brightman twins?' Sid, was always identified by the Foden Artic he drove for T. T. Boughtons, and John often ran with and loaded his brother with his Foden tractor and trailer. In fact, that was the only way some people could tell them apart. Sid joined the firm when he left school in 1927 and had thirty-six years on the road, thirty years of which were hauling from the West Country. An authoritative person once said, 'Sid Brightman has brought more timber up from Cornwall and Devon to the Home Counties than any other single driver', and few would dispute it. Such long term jobs took him from Looe to High Wycombe, and from Bodmin, Tavistock, and Barnstaple to places as far away as Park Royal in London and Malden in Essex.

The aftermath of the Lynmouth flood disaster saw Sid taking loads of girders down there and bringing timber back. Picturesque villages were ever a timber haulier's nightmare, as was Timberscombe in Somerset, where cottages overhung the narrow streets with only a foot to spare on each side. Sid recalled that the villagers would have to close any open windows before he could pass through the village.

If one innovation was greater than any other, it was the introduction of the twelve-speed gearbox. The worst hill on Bodmin Moor that previously took half an hour to ascend was done in twelve minutes with the aid of the new gearbox and with a similar load.

Carrying pre-cast concrete motorway bridge-beams at up to one hundred feet long came natural to Sid. A lifetime of long loads suited him well, and he spent his last five years carrying these vast loads across the country.

*The ERF Sid Brightman once drove*

*The Brightman twins*

*An average load for Sid*

*A wash and brush up*

*Sid Brightman near Looe*

# The Fensom Family

The brothers George and Albert Fensom of Friars Wash, Markyate, Herts, are well known for the immaculate maroon Matadors they run. Albert's pole trailer must be the last one operating for miles around. A leading veneer company ran a competition in the 'Farmer's Weekly' offering a prize to the farmer owning the biggest walnut tree. What a clever way to plot the largest walnuts in the country! The firm found them and Fensom's fetched them. For ten years the brothers travelled the country carrying prime walnut and oak veneer butts from Land's End to Norfolk, up to Jedburgh, around Shap, the Lakes, and every part of Wales.

But that's not how I remember Fensom's. Back in 1946, father, Jack Fensom, was hauling into Grove's sawmill at Tebworth in Bedfordshire. Two shortened Foden steam wagons with winches, similar to D types, brought huge loads in on old wooden-poled trailers, the boys acting as mates. Later, Albert was set up with a Mark 1 Latil No. JD8350, which has finished up her days at Beaulieu in Tate and Lyle livery, but less her anchors and winch. Today, you would never believe her working life was spent in timber. George took over an ex-USA 4 × 4 Federal artic. tractor unit. They replaced the fifth wheel with a Garwood winch and anchors. In due course, a Gardner 5 cylinder, a jib and air horns made her a very smart motor. She finally came out of service in 1966. Ironically, she has been standing in a quarry for over ten years, badly vandalized, with a tree growing through the chassis. She was sold at Christmas in 1983 for restoration and started after only a fifteen-yard snatch.

In one special way, Fensom's differ from any other hauliers I know. Jack Fensom set himself and the lads a high standard of professionalism regarding the appearance and turnout of his vehicles. He was not satisfied with the occasional wash and tidy up. These tractors were washed and polished with great regularity. When they were waiting to unload, and in any spare minute, the lads were always out with a rag and polish. I worked beside them for months. The tackle was always spotless despite their share of rough jobs. A common phrase today for any unmarked vehicle is 'In mint condition, ready to rally'. That's how Fensom's tackle went to work before rallies were ever thought of.

*George, Jack and Albert Fensom 1950's*

*Albert's Latil*

# Peter Mackinnon

I met Peter Mackinnon in a Churchyard where he was carrying out fine restoration work. We both were owners of and still used Unipowers it seemed. Ex-Cooper lads will remember this vehicle NBJ 661. Peter designed the four-in-line axle that winds up, when travelling along the road, to prevent tyre scrub. The lattice-jib raises and lowers on an independent winch. The machine is tested to lift eight tons. This is not uncommon in stone-masonry.

It is interesting to note that Peter's mother worked for the once well-known Saunderson Tractor Company where she braised radiators many years ago.

*The ex A.K. Cooper Unipower as she is today*

# Stan Sear

Stan Sear is an ex-Devon 'tree-trunker'. Vividly he described sites where a D6 could come out on to the road, be hooked on to his artic. unit and then drag him in backwards. With red Devon slurry only inches from the trailer-pole he'd load, and then the D6 would push or pull him out again.

Boarding the ferry at Torpoint was all right, but if the tide was low the ferry ramp would be steeper than usual with its surface always wet and slimy. A Quad was kept there just for towing off, but the sharp ramp incline would invariably cause the tree tails to rip the slats off the deck, to the almost hysterical fury of the ferrymen.

When Stan's destination was once changed after loading, his route involved a fourteen-foot bridge that his load would not clear. After seeing the length of the trees, the police explained that he would have to reverse over a mile to the nearest point wide enough to turn round. With a police car as escort, Stan did just this, completing the whole operation without having to draw forward to correct the unit at any stage. Nowadays, they rehearse for hours to perform similar but lesser feats at the 'Lorry Driver of the Year' events, but to Stan, it was all in a day's work. As with his father and brothers, steam and heavy tackle is in his blood.

*The AEC before the rebuild. Note the Petrol Autovac*

*Stan Sear with the famous rebuilt AEC and 7.7 diesel engine*
Reproduced by kind permission of Mr. John Boughton

108

# Bernard Berrows

Bernard Berrows of Oxford was not born in a Latil, but he was nursed and brought up in one. I saw a faded photograph of a canvas-topped Latil, timber carriage and living van with a woman standing on the steps, holding a babe in her arms. That babe was Bernard. At their inception over here, his father joined Latil UK and was Southern Area demonstrator. He went with Nobby, his loader mate, from timber merchant to sawmill across the South showing off the revolutionary little tractor that could do all that some steamers could, but in half the time and with a quarter of the ground damage. One could expect that the potential customer would find them the roughest trees on the wettest jobs, but even so the sales figures were very good for little daunted these men and machines. Bernard, the first of four children, lived in the van with his mother, but every week or so, she would ride in the narrow, open cab with her husband and Nobby, whilst Bernard reclined in a form of crib-cum-carrycot, made by his father, that fixed to the back bolster of the timber carriage.

Nobby excelled at loading and at catapulting; the odd pheasant feather always lingered in the cab. As Bernard grew up, it was a short stage from holding the wheel whilst on his father's lap to his little legs reaching the pedals, after which he drove in the fields. When he was five years old, his father changed his firm in order for the boy to get some schooling. As dad brought home a Latil at night, it was not long before Bernard, aged twelve, was taking the vehicle on the road for a joy-ride, after first making sure his parents had gone out, something he did several times without being caught, and only confessing this to his father twenty years later when he knew he would be less likely to get a thumping.

Whilst working for Timber and General Haulage in Sussex, his father was once on an estate when he broke a skid loading. Like the rest of us he took an axe to cut an ash pole for a new skid and was caught red-handed. This led to his instant dismissal. In two days, he was working for William Brown where he stayed until his retirement.

Bernard served with these two firms and with one or two others driving almost every make of timber vehicle. His photographs show that he was a proper member of the 'overhang gang', for his loads were often large, long and heavy, and from wet, bad sites. Moving large trees is in the blood of Bernard Berrows the Bolster Baby.

*One of the Latil Charcoal burners with Fred Bowler*

*Loading a "big one" at Apthorpe Park Brigstock*

*"Now that is a big tree" Kettering 1954*

*Ruts in the Bere Forest Hampshire*

110

*One of John Sadd's chain drive Foden*

111

# The Sadds

Two things stick in my mind about John Sadd and Sons of Maldon, Essex. One was the twisted nature of the trees I hauled from the West Country for them and the other was the deep sense of grief and shock that prevailed throughout the firm at the death of Alfred Sadd. Alfred, who had not sought the relative comfort and safety of the family business, had for years been a most successful Christian missionary in the Gilbert Islands far away in the Pacific, but had been shot by the Japanese. News had filtered through of the Japanese invasion and of his having been taken prisoner. He was one of the first to lay down his life for his faith.

John Sadd now eighty-seven was company chairman and joint managing director. The firm which was formed in 1730, was to become, at one time, one of our largest sawmills. Norman Sadd, now deceased, had managed the haulage. Even so, John Sadd could tell me that in 1871 a newspaper cutting read, "Mr. Sadd's Aveling and Porter traction engine destroyed the bridge at Battles Bridge owing to the bridge being insufficiently strong to take the load." His ancestors had the usual summons for black smoke and the frightening of animals.

After 1918, two ex-WD army surplus FWD petrol tractors proved a great success in timber haulage. During and for some time after both world wars the mill ran two eight-hour shifts cutting home-grown hardwoods as well as mahogany for boat skins and many other specialist requirements.

I remember the Foden and Douglas vehicles at Sadd's. One was a Douglas OPU3 whose winch jib, and anchors were removed for her to run as an artic. for some time. It was later converted back and I saw her recently at work in her native Essex.

In 1969, the company of John Sadd and Sons Ltd., was taken over by Boulton Paul (Joinery) Ltd. I am sure many readers will be pleased to know that Mr. John Sadd is fit and well in his eighty-seventh year.

*The ex Sadd Douglas 1983. (Fred Barton of Bishop Stortford ran her for 17 years. The 9.6 engine did 250,000 miles, high speeds diffs giving 60 mph)*

Although these photographs on this and the following three pages do not relate to any individual story, they are unique and cover a whole cross section of the many early forms of timber haulage.

*World War One Pagefield lorry*
Reproduced by kind permission of
The Forestry Commission

*Above and left:*
*T & A.J. Mann's unique*
*International, Earls Colne, Essex*

*Hauling near Hemel Hempstead*

Reproduced by the kind permission of
The Forestry Commission

113

*Holbrows of Bradford on Avon*

*"Chaining up" Holbrows Auto Tractor Model V*

*Auto mower winch*

*The Dartington Latil, at Totnes, Devon (1937). A footnote to this photograph read "It is regretted that this trailer carries only 10 tons, thus curtailing the payload, whilst fuel has now increased to 1/3³/₄ per gallon!"*

*A special load for the Foden (1930's)*

The above photographs reproduced by kind permission of Dartington Hall Trust.

*Edwin Foden would have been proud to see Jim Macdougall's 1946 fifty ton winch seen in Anglesey, May 1984.*
*"She's gorgeous!!"*

# Timber and elephants

The owner of two pet elephants was called up in 1941. The obvious answer to his problem was to offer them to the Home Timber Production Department. "Tongue in cheek" a fortnight's trial was offered in woods near Marlborough. Here the animals tushed and stacked well in the hands of their Indian trainer. However, the elephants became stubborn and awkward at others' attempts to handle them, and the whole idea fell through.

At Whipsnade "Dixie" is seen below loading the Citroen half track, a unique vehicle that would carry loads up the sheer face of the Downs proving invaluable in the early days of the Zoo.

Reproduced by kind permission of The Zoological Society of London

# A Challenge!

Could this be the oldest Unipower still at work?

New in 1940, it is seen here winching huge concrete structures from the River Severn in 1982.

# Give Thanks

Give thanks for the harvest of forest and field
Tall trees and fine timbers the wood that they yield
The fallers and hauliers who work with such skill
The chaps who deliver huge loads to the mill
From Noahs Ark to furnishings in your own home found
Give thanks for all timber — long may it abound.

Anon.